# The Best Life
## with
# Happiness

**PALMETTO**
PUBLISHING
Charleston, SC
www.PalmettoPublishing.com

Copyright © 2024 by Daniel K. Lee

All rights reserved

No portion of this book may be reproduced, stored in a retrieval system, or transmitted in any form by any means— electronic, mechanical, photocopy, recording, or other— except for brief quotations in printed reviews, without prior permission of the author.

Paperback ISBN: 9798822960206
eBook ISBN: 9798822970229

# The Best Life with Happiness

DANIEL K. LEE

# Table of Contents

**Section One: A Life Full of Joy** ............................................. 1
   1. The Miracle of Everyday Life ............................. 3
   2. Make Me Strong ................................................ 6
   3. A Life Full of Joy ............................................... 10
   4. Succeed Through Self-Development .................... 15
   5. The Wise and Beautiful Person ........................... 18
   6. The Joy of Salvation .......................................... 24

**Section Two: Love and Endless Love** ................................. 31
   7. Let's Walk with God .......................................... 33
   8. A Person like Light, A Person like Salt ................ 37
   9. Love and Endless Love ...................................... 41
  10. Grow with an Open Heart ................................. 47
  11. How to Improve Your Memory .......................... 51
  12. How to Manage Your Anger ............................... 54

**Section Three: The Eyes are The Lamp of The Heart** ....... 57
  13. Tapping into Good Habits ................................. 59
  14. Tearing Down the Tower of Babel Within Us ..... 63
  15. Always Be Grateful ............................................ 67
  16. Humbling Oneself Under God's Mighty Hand ... 71
  17. The Eyes Are the Lamp of the Heart .................. 76
  18. For the Lonely Soul ........................................... 79

**Section Four: The Power of Gratitude** ............................ 83
    19. Relationship between Science and Faith ............ 85
    20. Overcoming Trials ................................................ 90
    21. The Power of Gratitude ....................................... 94
    22. Let's pray even when we are busy ....................... 97
    23. The Path to a Prosperous Life .......................... 101
    24. Living with the End in Mind ............................ 104

**Section Five: Opening The Portal of Happiness** ........... 109
    25. Navigating Adversity: Finding Strength and Resilience ............................................................ 111
    26. God's Power through My Weakness ................. 114
    27. Choice of Thoughts, Power of Thoughts, and Value of Thoughts ........................................ 118
    28. New Year Wishes ............................................... 122
    29. The Sound of Spring ......................................... 125
    30. Opening the Portal of Happiness ..................... 127
    31. You Who Held My Hand .................................. 129
    32. Yesterday, Today, Tomorrow, and Time ............ 130

**About the Author** ........................................................ 132

# Preface

This book will greatly help you discover how to live a happy and meaningful life. Through decades of experience and trial and error, I have learned the way to live life most happily.

The key to living a happy life is living a life full of joy. In your relationship with yourself, cultivate consistent positive thoughts. In your relationships with others, build mutually amicable relationships. In your relationship with God, maintain a close relationship with the Lord and find comfort through His words and prayer. The principles for living a life full of joy are as follows: maintain humility and self-esteem in your relationship with yourself, share love and forgiveness in your relationships with others, and practice absolute faith and obedience in your relationship with God.

God desires for us to enjoy abundant joy and true happiness in this world. Ultimately, He wants us to become citizens of Heaven as His saved children. In our daily lives, we should experience miracles, strengthen our weaknesses through the Word and meditation, continually develop ourselves, and grow with an open mind. We must utilize good habits, dismantle our internal towers of Babel, and overcome difficult trials to build resilience and strength.

By humbling ourselves under God's mighty hand and living a life of constant prayer even in busy times, God's power will be revealed through our weaknesses. Let us embody a life of gratitude, comfort lonely souls, share continuous patience and unceasing love, and live wisely and beautifully as the salt and light of the world.

I hope that readers will live their lives well through a life full of joy and enjoy a more prosperous and abundant life. May the journey that begins now provide you with many insights and inspiration.

# Section One:
## A Life Full of Joy

# 1.
# The Miracle of Everyday Life

Even the simple act of waking up and breathing every morning is a miracle because the gift of life within us allows us to live with joy, gratitude, and passionate hope. As we go through each day, finding meaning in the small things allows us to experience special and unique moments. Whether we are happy or sad, spending time with others, loving and helping each other, sharing emotions, encouraging one another, and creating memories show just how precious and wondrous life is

Everything we hold dear, every moment we have lived, reveals the miraculous nature of life. We are always connected with nature, and our daily interactions and routines are closely linked with it. Our hearts rise and set like the sun, wax and wane like the moon. These phenomena are not mere coincidences but precious gifts from nature. Moreover, nature communicates with us through gentle whispers. The melody of the wind blowing through the pine trees, the lively chirping of birds in the bushes, the peaceful murmuring of a stream in the valley—these experiences highlight the everyday miracles surrounding us. The changing hues of sunrise and sunset, the cyclical transformation of the seasons—all remind us of the wonders of everyday life. Likewise, our very existence—the ability to breathe, dream, and live—is a miracle in itself.

Life is a constant challenge. In my early thirties, I experienced the devastating loss of my business and all my possessions in a fire. However, as I navigated through this adversity, I discovered my resilience and inner strength, and I consider overcoming this a miracle. Such trials nurtured the vigor of youth and ignited passionate dreams for a brighter future. Through trials, we gain perseverance, character, and hope, and realizing hope through trials is the miracle of our lives.

Recognizing the importance of these everyday miracles, when we cultivate a deep sense of gratitude for each moment, we realize that life itself is a precious gift and that miracles are woven into the fabric of our daily experiences. Miracles always happen in everyday life, and the ability to live each day with gratitude is a miracle.

When we develop the ability to find miracles in our memories and in the present moment, we experience new wonders every day. This makes our lives more beautiful and enriching, and it makes each moment more precious. The everyday miracles are the small moments we can feel daily, through which we come to appreciate the preciousness and gratitude of life. Harmony with nature, precious time with people, and inner growth gained through adversity are all part of the miracle. As long as our lives continue, recognizing and being grateful for these miracles is true happiness.

# 2.
# Make Me Strong

Like the face of Janus, we humans possess dual minds, rendering us simultaneously strong and weak, positive and negative, bright and cheerful yet dark and depressed, good and evil. To those of us who are fragile like earthenware and weak like reeds, the Lord says, "Strengthen the weak hands, and make firm the feeble knees" (Isaiah 35:3). Within us exists a constant struggle between the desire to satisfy our egos and the fear that arises from our environment and circumstances. When we succumb to these psychological conflicts, we become weak.

Amidst the flood of material civilization, mental poverty, and a lack of values that prioritize materialism, pleasure, and comfort over the dignity of life leave people emotionally unstable. This leads to a sense of self-loss, social isolation, despair, emptiness, and ultimately makes them weaker. These negative thoughts and weak minds hinder our willpower and diminish our strength and resilience. To strengthen myself, I must consistently move forward with patience and perseverance, embracing positive thoughts and a broad mind, relying on the Lord with a spirit of challenge, courage, and conviction.

To attain strength, we must cultivate a broad mind that encompasses infinite possibilities. When we possess vision and an open mind, our thoughts are not confined to a closed triangle; rather, they are similar to the Kanizsa triangle, an open triangle that can be infinitely expanded by adding three Pac-Man shapes. By expanding the virtual space within us, we unlock boundless possibilities. Consider the hummingbird, one of the smallest birds in the world, measuring only 6 cm in length. Despite its diminutive size, it is among the toughest birds. It sustains itself by extracting nectar from flowers while hovering in mid-air. Due to this demanding lifestyle, the average lifespan of a hummingbird is merely four years. On the other hand, we have the albatross, the largest bird, capable of flying the highest and farthest distances, spanning from the North to the South Poles. These birds have an average lifespan of 40 to 50 years, with some living up to 85 years. The secret to their long-distance flight lies in dynamic soaring and gliding. They seek out storms, launching themselves from high cliffs into the raging winds. They spread their wings, soaring to the pinnacle of the storm, and when the winds subside, they glide great distances. These birds derive 98% of their energy for flight from the wind, with only 2% expended on wing flapping. Similarly, like hummingbirds, we can live by relying solely on our abilities. And like albatrosses, we can draw strength from nature, entrusting everything to God and living within the power He grants us. By relying on the Lord and embracing infinite possibilities, expanding our horizons, and approaching life with unwavering courage and enthusiasm, we can cultivate strength.

Furthermore, when we find ourselves weak, we must persevere and move forward with patience. As Cervantes said, "Rome was not built in a day," impatience is a major obstacle for us. We must adopt a long-term view and be patient. Thomas Carlyle, the author of The History of the French Revolution, spent ten years preparing the first draft of this book. He then entrusted the review to his good friend John Stuart Mill. Unfortunately, a bundle of manuscripts was burned due to a maid's mistake. Initially discouraged, Carlyle stopped eating and drinking, but eventually found the strength to resume writing the manuscript through sheer will and perseverance. Even in despair, his unwavering tenacity made his work an eternal masterpiece. It is said that bees must gather nectar from 56,000 flowers to produce one pound of honey. Like fruits that ripen under the scorching sun and rice that only bears fruit after a long period of time, we also need effort, patience, and time to turn weaknesses into strengths. Constantly honing our skills and engaging in self-improvement are crucial.

Lastly, when we are weak, we must embrace challenges with courage and conviction. Thomas Edison, who endured 200 failures before achieving one successful invention, firmly believed that the distinction between 'difficult' and 'impossible' lay solely in the amount of time required. With his unwavering spirit of perseverance, he contributed greatly to mankind, having made over 1,300 inventions. Edison famously proclaimed, "The surest path to success is to try again." The spirit of challenge encompasses the audacious actions that shape history and enable individuals to live a positive life.

The core of civilization is not stagnant; rather, it continuously shifts and evolves. Rome, once a modest city-state on the banks of the Tiber, conquered Greece, a formidable power that had previously subjugated the Persian Empire. Rome triumphed over its archenemy, Carthage, and established a vast empire centered around the Mediterranean Sea. This serves as an exemplification of strategic development, as history has witnessed the dominion of the strong over the weak. The Lord assures us, "Fear not, for I am with you; be not dismayed, for I am your God; I will strengthen you, I will help you, I will uphold you with my righteous right hand" (Isaiah 41:10). He encourages us to fortify our feeble hands with courage and faith.

When we firmly anchor our faith in God, adopt an expansive mindset with limitless possibilities, persist with unwavering determination and resilience, and embrace a life of challenges, courage, and confidence, we can emerge stronger and lead triumphant lives.

# 3.
# A Life Full of Joy

The inner beauty of human beings is manifested through joy. A person who is grateful for even the smallest things is happy and full of joy. God desires for us to always rejoice and live. Those who possess joy become carriers of the happiness virus, spreading joy to others. When in the company of joyful individuals, joy overflows and permeates the atmosphere. Conversely, if we surround ourselves with individuals harboring anger and resentment, our joy can be diminished. Living our daily lives in a state of joy is a constant challenge.

Human beings experience a range of emotions, including joy, anger, sadness, love, hate, and greed. The Bible specifically addresses joy and sorrow, stating, "A joyful heart is good medicine, but a crushed spirit dries up the bones" (Proverbs 17:22). Joy strengthens our souls, while sorrow weakens them. Furthermore, the Bible advises, "Make no friendship with a man given to anger, nor go with a wrathful man, lest you learn his ways and entangle yourself in a snare" (Proverbs 22:25). The reason is that the angry and embittered can rob us of our joy, subject us to tests, and entangle us in traps.

Now, let's explore three ways to sustain lasting joy and maintain its fullness.

Firstly, in order to preserve joy, it is crucial to cultivate positive thoughts consistently.

Each day, we must embrace the belief that good things will happen and anticipate moments of happiness. To achieve this, we must cultivate a positive mindset, carefully tending to the field of our hearts and sowing seeds of positive thoughts. For example, as children of God, if we approach every aspect of life with optimism and pride, we will possess bright, happy, and joyful hearts. We should remember that God sees us not as weak and humble, but as warriors. God instructs us, "Be strong and courageous, do not be afraid, for I will be with you wherever you go." As God's children, we must always bear in mind that we are warriors of God.

Let us strive to embrace positive thoughts such as, "God wants to bless and protect me. He wants His face to shine upon me, showering me with His grace. God loves me unconditionally, and nothing can rob me of my joy." This mindset fosters peace and happiness, ensuring our ongoing happiness.

In criminology, the "broken windows theory," presented by James Wilson and George Kelling, posits that if a building owner neglects a broken window, children or passersby may throw stones and break more windows, increasing the likelihood of further crimes such as theft and robbery. The same principle applies to economics and psychology. If negative thoughts enter our minds, we must swiftly dismiss them. Complaints, dissatisfaction, distrust, anxiety, worry, irritation, hatred, jealousy, arrogance, frustration, and fear are akin to broken windows. When such thoughts infiltrate our minds, they often bring temporary pleasure, leading to doubt, surrender to temptation, and engagement in destructive actions. They sow trouble in our lives and steal away our joy. This is why God consistently urges us to rejoice. By driving out negative thoughts and diligently sowing seeds of joy in our hearts, we enable those seeds to grow and bear abundant fruits of joy. Consequently, our hearts become filled with joy.

Secondly, to consistently maintain inner joy, it is essential to cultivate positive relationships with others.

We coexist with our neighbors in various settings such as our homes, churches, workplaces, and communities. These encounters provide us with the opportunity to support and uplift one another, thereby enriching our lives with joy. By treating others with respect, appreciating their worth, and embracing a friendly disposition towards our neighbors, we create an atmosphere that fosters happiness. To foster good relationships, it is important to refrain from engaging in arguments, show respect to others, initiate friendly conversations, elicit positive responses, and empathize with their perspectives and desires. Through a heartfelt approach that respects and considers others, we not only cultivate amicable relationships but also establish strong connections. Consequently, individuals who prioritize building positive relationships, demonstrating respect, and considering others can lead lives brimming with joy.

Thirdly, to consistently maintain joy, it is crucial to live a life closely connected to the Lord, seeking solace in His Word and through prayer.

Similar to how a weak branch must be grafted onto a tree with strong roots to bear good fruit, we, as feeble branches, find true purpose and hope when we rely on and seek refuge in God—the tree with unwavering roots. This act of grafting is a profound aspect of faith. By maintaining proximity to the Lord through reading His Word and engaging in prayer, we transform from wild olive trees into true olive trees. Even in the face of adversity and challenging circumstances, when we entrust everything to the Lord, the Holy Spirit consoles our hearts, allowing us to find joy in any situation.

Genuine joy emanates from the Lord. As the giver of life, He serves as the source and reason for our joy. Joy is a divine gift bestowed upon us, serving as the driving force behind our lives. Authentic joy can only be attained through a relationship with the Lord. When we express gratitude in our prayers and immerse ourselves in His Word, living in close communion with Him, we can lead lives overflowing with joy.

In conclusion, to consistently experience a life full of joy, it is imperative to incorporate three key elements: cultivating positive thoughts, nurturing meaningful relationships with others, and maintaining a close connection to the Lord through His Word and prayer. By adhering to these principles, we will live as individuals who radiate abundant joy.

# 4.
# Succeed Through Self-Development

Life is an ongoing journey of learning, and self-development plays a crucial role in bringing about positive changes in our lives. By honing our talents and abilities through self-development, we become better equipped to achieve our goals and aspirations. Additionally, it empowers us to take control of our lives and shape the future we desire. Self-development is essential for nurturing our inherent abilities and leading a more enriching and meaningful life. However, many individuals are unaware of their own potential.

To gain a scientific understanding of human behavior, the field of psychology explores the conscious processes and behaviors of individuals, aiding us in comprehending our own minds as well as those of others. Psychology employs research methods like observation, experimentation, and investigation to gather scientific and objective data. By uncovering the principles that govern human behavior, psychology aims to enhance the quality of human life.

Embracing self-development through psychology yields numerous advantages. It fosters self-awareness, facilitating a deeper understanding of our thoughts, personality, senses, perceptions, and behaviors. It acknowledges that human thinking and perception are influenced by contexts, perspectives, evaluation criteria, and assumptions. Self-development equips us with effective techniques and skills to bolster our personal strengths, such as cultivating hope, envisioning success, embracing positive thinking, managing stress, and developing inner resilience. It empowers individuals to enhance self-confidence, pursue opportunities, embrace challenges with a growth mindset, and accomplish their objectives.

Overall, self-development through psychology empowers individuals to lead fulfilling lives, forge meaningful relationships, unlock their full potential, and develop beneficial habits through continuous practice. "The beginning of wisdom is this: Get wisdom, and whatever you get, get insight." (Proverbs 4:7). These words highlight the significance of wisdom and emphasize its importance in our lives.

The seven psychological laws of success, providing a powerful framework for personal development, are The Law of Control, The Law of Cause and Effect, The Law of Belief,

The Law of Expectations, The Law of Attraction, The Law of Correspondence, and The Law of Mental Equivalency.

Through self-development, the wisdom of self-awareness and the wisdom of understanding the world shape our future, while our intuition guides us on the path ahead in life. To enhance the success rate of personal growth, it is beneficial to maintain constant motivation, cultivate the habit of taking notes, develop leadership skills, and foster relationships with others to provide mutual support and encouragement. When we broaden our perspective, we gain clarity, and with an open mind, new opportunities present themselves. To win someone's heart, it is important to empathize and see things from their point of view. Trusting others is a key aspect of gaining their trust. Our values act as a compass, guiding our actions. Ultimately, a fulfilling life emphasizes essence and seeks balance. True victory lies in conquering oneself.

# 5.
# The Wise and Beautiful Person

People who are wise and good can make life wonderful. They are beautiful in their thoughts and words. They lead a life of gratitude and preparedness, always ready to do good with wisdom and humility. Such a person bears good fruit, avoids envy and conflict, and strives to be a peacemaker. According to the Bible, "The good man brings good things out of the good stored up in his heart, and the evil man brings evil things out of the evil stored up in his heart." Let us delve into the characteristics of a wise and virtuous individual.

First and foremost, wise and beautiful people have beautiful thoughts.

Our thoughts shape our future, and everything stems from our thinking. No one can make us unhappy as long as we perceive ourselves as happy. It is not fate that dictates our lives but rather the belief that our future can be altered. Pascal, renowned for his statement, "Man is a thinking reed," wrote in his book Pensées, "Human beings were created to think, and human dignity and worth lie in thinking, and the human task is to think when thinking." Positive thinking is a thing of beauty. It acts as a remedy, promoting physical well-being and instilling dreams and hopes that promise a bright future even in the face of adversity, persecution, or tribulation.

Joshua and Caleb, who explored the land of Canaan, exemplified individuals with positive thoughts. While the other ten spies saw the Canaanites as giants and declared that they could not conquer the land, Joshua and Caleb held a positive perspective. Those who seek wisdom are profound thinkers. Wisdom flows ceaselessly like water from the depths of Ongdalsaem, surpassing the limits of human knowledge, judgment, concentration, and memory. The Bible states, "Get wisdom, get understanding; do not forget my words or turn away from them. Do not forsake wisdom, and she will protect you; love her, and she will watch over you."

A life of spiritual growth entails meditating on the Word of God daily, gaining wisdom, and becoming deeply rooted in the Scriptures. Proverbs 30 reveals that there are four small yet wise creatures on Earth: the ant, which lacks strength but prepares food in summer; the badger, which is feeble but builds its nest among rocks; the locust, which has no king but swarms together; and the lizard, which can be caught by hand yet resides in palaces. These creatures teach the foolish and unwise to acquire wisdom. Just as iron sharpens iron and a person brightens their friend's face, walking with the wise leads to wisdom.

Next, wise and beautiful people have beautiful speech.

Words possess immense power, capable of giving life or causing harm. They can inspire dreams and hopes, but they can also incite frustration and despair. Some people express resentment and complaints, while others choose to convey gratitude, positivity, and love. In 2004, actor Christopher Reeve, known for his portrayal of Superman, passed away. He was once regarded as the embodiment of Superman, a hero who solved all problems with his extraordinary abilities. Ironically, he found himself unable to perform even the most basic tasks. He couldn't chew food or urinate without assistance, relying solely on a ventilator to stay alive. Faced with the choice of either living in his deteriorated state or seeking euthanasia to avoid displaying his own helplessness, Christopher Reeve pleaded with doctors to end his life. However, his wife, Dana, firmly refused, uttering a single word that changed everything: "You." She said, "While you are alive, you are still you! It's still you!" In that one word, she conveyed a message of unwavering support, hope, and love. Dana's words saved a life and resurrected the spirit of Superman. Following this incident, Christopher Reeve delved into extraordinary realms. He established the non-profit Christopher Reeve Foundation, which made significant contributions to spinal nerve regeneration research. Until his departure, he embodied the essence of a true Superman, accomplishing remarkable feats.

One's words possess boundless hope, courage, and vitality. God created the heavens and the earth with His Word, which holds a living and active power. Similarly, the words spoken by those who live in the Lord possess the ability to heal and shape the future. Those who bless others with words of grace, faith, hope, healing, gratitude, and love are truly wise and beautiful individuals.

Additionally, wise and beautiful people care for others, live harmoniously, and consistently express gratitude.

Living a self-centered existence, solely concerned with oneself, leads to entanglement with thorns. Conversely, those who demonstrate kindness become farmers who yield plentiful crops in fertile soil. Those who possess the ability to perceive understand the importance of uplifting others. Our society flourishes and experiences greater happiness through warm hearts rather than material wealth. It is often said that true success lies in the act of giving, and a benevolent person receives the gratitude of others regardless of their status or possessions. When one lives by considering their neighbors, they can enjoy a peaceful life alongside them. Life offers countless reasons to be grateful. Gratitude deepens our awareness that we are not contingent beings but rather God's chosen children. Although we cannot predict the future, knowing that God is with us frees us from worries. Conversely, a lack of gratitude and excessive complaints only fuel anxiety and cloud our judgment, corroding both the mind and body. It is unwise to dwell on future worries while neglecting to live well in the present. The realm of faith liberates us from worries, enabling us to perceive everything anew. It grants us gratitude, joy, and peace. A person who appreciates even the smallest things is genuinely happy.

Lastly, wise and beautiful people praise the Lord and lead prepared lives.

The beauty of those who sing praises and let their souls soar is as radiant as the morning sun and as gentle as the fragrance of flowers in a garden. "Make a joyful noise to the Lord, all the earth! Serve the Lord with gladness! Come into his presence with singing! Know that the Lord, he is God! It is he who made us, and we are his; we are his people, and the sheep of his pasture. Enter his gates with thanksgiving, and his courts with praise! Give thanks to him; bless his name!" (Psalms 100:1-4)

When we praise the Lord, grace fills our souls with joy and peace. Even amidst sorrow, pain, and despair, praising the Lord evokes overwhelming gratitude for His eternal goodness and loving-kindness. Furthermore, wise individuals lead prepared lives. None of us knows when the Lord will call us or when He will return—whether it be day or night. In Matthew 25, Jesus shared the parable of the ten virgins, five of whom were wise and prepared with oil for their lamps to meet the bridegroom and join the wedding feast. Similar to the foolish rich man who declared, "Soul, you have ample goods laid up for many years; relax, eat, drink, be merry," God responded, saying, "Fool! This night your soul is required of you, and the things you have prepared, whose will they be?" Thus, we must live wisely and prepare ourselves, embracing the hope of heaven.

To sum up, wise and beautiful people possess beautiful thoughts and speak beautifully. They live in harmony with their neighbors, always praising the Lord in a life of gratitude. They lead prepared lives and strive to glorify God in all they do. Their virtuous deeds have a positive impact on others, illuminating the world like a beacon in the darkness. The more wise and beautiful individuals there are, the brighter the world becomes.

# 6.
# The Joy of Salvation

We are moved by the grace of the Lord, who saved us from the path of death and brought us onto the path of life. Every time we lift up the cup of salvation and praise the Lord, our souls are revived. It is through the Lord's great grace that we experience this joy.

Among all the graces bestowed upon us by God, the greatest is the forgiveness of our sins and the salvation from death to life. The blessings and gifts that flow from the depths of our souls—joy and gratitude, love and peace, comfort and hope, dreams and courage—are given to those who are saved by the Lord.

"What shall I render to the Lord for all his benefits to me? I will lift up the cup of salvation and call on the name of the Lord," (Psalms 116:12-13).

The best way we, as children of God, can show our gratitude is by exalting the cup of salvation above all else and praising the Lord.

In the past, there were times when we turned away from the Lord and wandered in darkness, unsure of which path to take. There were moments when our souls wandered through valleys of despair and discouragement, falling into pain and futility. Those who wander in darkness often seek solace by imitating the ways of the world. However, wrong imitations can destroy lives, leading individuals to drink from the "cup of wrath."

A notable example of the destructive power of wrong imitation is evident in the aftermath of Johann Wolfgang von Goethe's novel, "The Sorrows of Young Werther." After its publication, a significant number of young people in Europe tragically committed suicide, mimicking the protagonist's suicide. This demonstrates how Werther's influence did not save people but rather destroyed them, compelling them to drink from the "cup of wrath."

The fact that we are saved means we can never live a life of failure; instead, we are destined to live as victors. This victorious life stems from recognizing that the work we are given each day is bestowed upon us by the Lord. When we live with zeal, even in the smallest of tasks, that work glorifies God. Only the victorious can raise the cup of salvation.

Those who possess the joy of salvation lift up the cup of salvation and glorify the Lord. This cup represents the life of

Jesus dwelling within us, the grace freely given to us by God, the hope that plants dreams and visions, and the dedication to serve humbly.

The cup of salvation symbolizes the life in which Jesus resides within us.

If we open Fyodor Dostoevsky's work, "The Brothers Karamazov," we encounter the following sentence on the first page: "Take care. If a grain of wheat does not fall to the ground and die, it remains as it is. If it dies, it bears much fruit." This quotation is a verse from the Gospel of John (12:24). One of the central messages of this work, which aims to reconcile the conflicting principles of good and evil, is how to lead a righteous human life.

Jesus became a grain of wheat to save all of humanity, and likewise, our lives must also become grains of wheat, fulfilling the roles of light and salt in the world. The cup of salvation represents the life where Jesus lives within us through His sacrifice on the cross. When we believe in Jesus, we are saved, and the fundamental problems of our lives are resolved. As beings incapable of achieving anything on our own, we gain salvation and spiritual authority and power by living with the Lord, who is the way, the truth, and the life. Furthermore, when we live as grains of wheat, playing our part as lights and salt in the world, we experience the joy of salvation and gain eternal life.

The cup of salvation is the cup of grace freely given to us by God.

How can we express the immeasurable grace of the Lord? Consider the following analogy: Jesus once said in Matthew 18 that even if we cannot forgive our neighbor a hundred denarii, the Lord has forgiven us ten thousand talents, which is six hundred thousand times more than we can ever give. We raise the cup of salvation in gratitude for this grace. When we wholeheartedly strive each day, we can lead successful lives through God's grace. We raise the cup of salvation because we are exhilarated by the grace of the Lord, who guides our lives each day, and because we possess the joy of salvation.

The cup of salvation is the cup of hope.

Hope is the light that illuminates the dark hearts of human beings. Allow me to provide an example. "The Star-Spangled Banner," the American national anthem composed by Francis Scott Key, sings of hope amidst despair. One day in 1814, as American and British troops engaged in battle, Key witnessed the American flag proudly flying over Fort McHenry in Baltimore. This sight filled his heart with hope as he emerged from the depths of frustration and despair in the pitch-black night. The anthem eloquently expresses this sentiment:

"O say can you see, by the dawn's early light/ Whose broad stripes and bright stars through the perilous fight/ Gave proof through the night that our flag was still there/ O'er the land of the free and the home of the brave/ Tis the Star-Spangled Banner, oh long may it wave!/ And the Star-Spangled Banner in triumph doth/ O thus be it ever when freemen shall stand/ Praise the power that hath made and preserved us a nation."

Hope grants dreams for the future and nurtures visions, much like a flag adorned with stars. We raise the cup of salvation high because it represents the joy of salvation, where the Lord bestows hope and vision upon us, even in times of despair and frustration.

The cup of salvation is the cup of humble dedication to service.

Pierre-Auguste Renoir, a world-renowned French painter of the 19th century, was an Impressionist artist. Due to his impoverished upbringing, he worked in a pottery factory from a young age. Immersed in the study of color and painting, he continued his artistry even when afflicted with neuralgia, drawing with a brush in his hand when his hand could no longer hold it. Renoir once stated, "When an artist believes he has talent, it is his downfall. When he sets aside his pride and diligently works like a humble weaver, his art can flourish." It was his humble heart that propelled him to become a world-class painter.

As Jesus said, "Take my yoke upon you and learn from me, for I am gentle and humble in heart, and you will find rest for your souls" (Matthew 11:29). When we live with meek and humble hearts, the Lord will exalt us in due time. We raise the cup of salvation because the joy of salvation resides in living a life devoted to humble service according to the Lord's will.

In summary, the cup of salvation represents the life where Jesus dwells within us, the grace freely given to us by God, the hope that plants dreams and visions, and the dedication to serve humbly. Lord, we express our gratitude for being able to live with the joy of salvation. As we journey with You each day, we lift up the cup of salvation and worship You. We raise the cup of life, the cup of grace, the cup of hope, and the cup of devotion to praise You. As we walk with You daily, lifting up the cup of salvation, we give glory to You, who has bestowed upon us the joy of salvation.

# Section Two:
## Love and Endless Love

# 7.
# Let's Walk with God

Sunflowers thrive by facing the sun, and fish swim freely in the water. Similarly, the earth revolves and rotates around the sun. Just as everything in the universe has a center, humans cannot sustain life without God, the Creator. The carnal mind leads to death, while the spiritual mind brings life and peace.

    Life can be likened to a ship sailing through the vast ocean, striving to reach its destination. Sometimes, we encounter strong winds, turbulent waves, and fierce rainstorms. Other times, the journey is smooth. In this troubled world, we must have confidence in the belief that God is always by our side. We must trust in God from beginning to end, as this trust grants us the courage and confidence to overcome any trials and tribulations that come our way.

Negative thinking, discouragement, and weakness hinder our progress and diminish our ability to solve challenging problems. If we perceive ourselves as weak and insignificant, we will only become such individuals. Conversely, if we embrace our identity as children of God with humility and pride, we will possess the capability to conquer any difficulties. We have the potential for possibility, the power to create, the capacity for dreams, the pursuit of pleasure, the courage to triumph, the abundance of victory, the tranquility of peace, and the fulfillment of success. Those who maintain a positive mindset, focusing on happiness, lead victorious lives.

Even when facing adversity, we must hold onto hope and maintain a vision for the future while unwavering in our faith in God's greatness. God is the absolute ruler of the world, eternal, omnipresent, omnipotent, and unchanging. Such a God is our Father, and we are His children. It is crucial to remember that God sees us as strong and courageous individuals. We must find contentment in the way God created us, recognizing that He has endowed each person with the appropriate appearance, talent, and character. When we give our best efforts, we will receive astounding blessings poured out by God, leading to a successful life prepared for us.

Even a dying branch can be revitalized, nourished, and bear fruit when attached to a robust tree. Similarly, when we cling to and rely on God, the tree with unyielding roots, we can attain true life and experience a peaceful existence.

It is not our circumstances that trip us up, but rather our negative thoughts about them. These thoughts lead us to ruin, leaving us defeated and frustrated. We must exercise caution when associating with individuals who disregard God's grace and adopt a negative outlook. We should not allow ourselves to be influenced by their pessimistic attitudes toward life. Mephibosheth, the grandson of Saul, referred to himself as a "dead dog" with a lame leg, and the ten spies whom Moses sent to Canaan compared themselves to a "swarm of locusts," belittling their own capabilities. These individuals had self-portraits of defeat, and as a result, they experienced actual defeat. We must remember that God sees us as warriors.

Always keep positive examples from the Bible in mind. Seeking advice from respected individuals when faced with difficult decisions or uncertain choices is beneficial. Discouragement, destructive thoughts, fears, worries, doubts, and insecurities have no place in our relationship with God. When these thoughts arise, we must promptly dismiss them. Our enemies reside within our hearts. We must change our thinking, adopting a mindset that centers on God in all things. Let go of the past and press forward. Even if our present circumstances are filled with hardships and adversities, we must not abandon the belief that God is with us.

When we embrace "God's perspective," viewing life through His eyes and focusing on His will, He will witness our faith and accomplish astounding works. We must not allow the demands, pressures, and excessive expectations of others to hinder us from fulfilling God's desires. Engaging in actions we don't desire to avoid hurting others only leads to self-deception. We should strive to maintain consistency in our behavior, whether at work, home, or in our interactions with neighbors and friends.

Let us pursue a positive and joyful life with hearts filled with brightness and happiness. In doing so, we will attract happy, joyful, and positive individuals into our lives. As children of God, we must always remain humble, embracing both humility and pride. This will attract individuals who possess the same humility and pride. By utilizing our wisdom, experience, knowledge, and other abilities within the framework of God's will, He will guide us onto the path of righteousness.

# 8.
# A Person like Light, A Person like Salt

Since humans are social animals, their lives differ depending on the kind of society and environment they live in. Therefore, fostering a better environment and promoting an orderly world are essential for improving the quality of life. Many believe that God wants us to live as sources of light and salt in the world.

Light allows us to perceive our surroundings, with the sun being the primary visible light source around us. All light originates from atoms, which emit light by absorbing energy from other sources or colliding with other particles. For instance, the sun shines because nuclear reactions between hydrogen atoms in its nucleus release a significant amount of energy. Conversely, darkness results from the absence of light.

As our advanced scientific civilization develops rapidly, the world seems to be succumbing to increasing materialism, corruption, and darkness caused by excessive indulgence in pleasure, dishonesty, temptation, and crime. The more people's hearts grow callous, the greater the need for individuals who can act as beacons of light, shining positivity and goodness upon the world. A person who radiates light is someone who becomes a beacon of positivity and exerts a positive and influential impact on others.

Fanny Jane Crosby (1820-1915) wrote 23 of her hymns and penned more than 9,000 hymns throughout her lifetime. At the age of six months, she became blind due to a doctor's mistake. When she turned 30, she heard the hymn "What Wondrous Love Is This?" and underwent a conversion. Since then, she made significant contributions by writing numerous hymn poems. She couldn't see the world with her eyes, but she lived as a lamp, shedding light on the world.

When people expressed sympathy for her inability to see, Fanny responded, "I thank God. I am so grateful to think that when I go to heaven, I will have the opportunity to see the Lord I love with my newfound eyesight." This exemplifies a life lived as a beacon of light.

Salt is a substance with a salty taste, primarily composed of NaCl. Salt exists in bodily fluids and is vital for humans and animals as it plays a crucial role in maintaining osmotic pressure. Salt's role extends to preserving and preventing food from spoiling while imparting flavor. The average salt concentration in seawater is 3.5%, which prevents it from rotting.

Throughout human history, salt has symbolized wealth, power, and currency. Some argue that Rome was able to become a great empire because of its ability to control salt. Even today, in the outskirts of Rome, there is a road called 'Via Salaria,' meaning 'Salt Road.' The highest praise during the Roman era was being described as 'a person like the salt of the world.' The words "soldier" and "salad" both stem from the prefix "sal," which is related to salt. The term "salary" refers to payment, and the expression "salaryman" also originates from this root.

When salt loses its taste, it becomes useless. Salt dissolves wherever it is needed, benefiting all substances. The taste of salt is experienced only when it dissolves, and it is valued for its selflessness. A person like salt positively influences others through love, consideration, dedication, hope, and sacrifice. When we do our best for our neighbors and the world, we make a positive impact, and the best comes back to us. This obeys the law of cause and effect, whereby our actions produce consequences that are reflected in us.

British philosopher Francis Bacon (1561-1626) once described three archetypes of individuals. Firstly, he referred to those who resemble spiders: individuals endowed with remarkable talents but employ them to deceive, conspire, harm, and exploit others. Secondly, he depicted those akin to ants: self-centered individuals who toil diligently to fulfill their own needs, disregarding the welfare of others. Lastly, Bacon identified individuals akin to bees. Bees are individuals who not only lead fulfilling lives through hard work but also bring benefits to others.

People who resemble light and salt, akin to bees, lead blessed lives, bring about positive change in others, and exert a beneficial influence. Those who are like light radiate through their unwavering principles and strong sense of identity, becoming beacons of inspiration to the world. Beings like salt take care of others' wounds with a warm heart, instill hope, and show affection by sacrificing themselves. Just as light continues to shine, and salt preserves its taste, when we live as individuals who resemble light and salt, we will have a positive influence on the world. Therefore, we can lead a happy and prosperous life filled with joy and gratitude.

# 9.
# Love and Endless Love

The etymology of the English word "love," which means affection or deep care, can be traced back to the Latin word 'Lubere,' meaning 'to rejoice.' It is a feeling of immense happiness that arises when one meets that special person, encompassing the true essence of love.

Love is undoubtedly one of the most common human emotions, but it can also be acknowledged as a complex and subtle emotion. The mere presence of this feeling for someone can bring immense joy, leading one to hold the person in high regard.

Eric Fromm once aptly stated, "Love is like a meal. If it is not continually nourished, it may diminish due to inadequacy." When experiencing love, the brain releases several chemicals, including pheromones, dopamine, norepinephrine, serotonin, oxytocin, and vasopressin.

From birth, humans are often seen as solitary beings, and due to their capacity for thought, they tend to safeguard themselves through various means. One of the most significant methods is through different forms of cooperation with others, and love stands as the most important form of such cooperation. Parental love, brotherly love, heterosexual love, friendship, religious love, and romantic love are among the many kinds of love. However, it is important to note that human beings cannot overcome their loneliness with just one form of love. Loneliness has been an intrinsic part of human existence, as has the love between opposite sexes. As such, the nature of humans as solitary beings becomes a pivotal factor in the formation of romantic relationships.

Sternberg's theory identifies three fundamental components of love: intimacy, commitment, and passion.

1. Intimacy: This involves warmth and a close connection, where individuals share their innermost selves in a relationship.
2. Commitment: It is the conscious intention to continue the relationship despite the challenges and sacrifices that may arise.
3. Passion: This component represents the intense physical and sexual desire felt for the other person.

Plato, in his classification of love, defines four types: Eros (physical love), Philia (brotherly love), Ludus (playful love), and Agape (unconditional love). According to Plato, love evolves from carnal desire to unconditional love over time.

Now, let's delve into a more detailed classification of the types of love, encompassing eight categories:

1. Eros: This is romantic love, entirely driven by physical attraction and the enchantment of sexual desire. Such love often burns intensely but may also fade quickly.
2. Ludus: Ludus refers to playful and casual love. The individuals involved may not display deep interest in each other, but they enjoy each other's company and find the relationship fun and exciting. There might not be a mutual exchange of intense emotions, but the relationship is appreciated for its lightheartedness.
3. Storge: Storge is a love that exists between family members, primarily within immediate family relationships. However, it can also be experienced among members of the same tribe or people fulfilling a common mission or duty.
4. Philia: Philia represents fraternal love or friendship. It is a state of pure-hearted caring for the well-being of the other person, often seen when friendship deepens into love.
5. Mania: Mania denotes possessive and passionate love. It is characterized by an intense desire and even obsession for the other person, which can lead to moments of madness and impulsiveness. However, this type of love may be prone to sudden destruction.
6. Pragma: Pragma signifies practical and realistic love. It is a love where reason and compatibility precede emotions. People in such relationships love each other because they are

well-suited in many ways, leading to the development of a profound connection over time.
7. Agape: Agape embodies selfless love, often associated with Christian ideals. It is a love that thrives through concessions, understanding, and sacrifices. Agape is the foundational concept of platonic love, although it might be challenging to find in its purest form in reality.
8. Philautia: Philautia represents self-love. It is not a negative or unhealthy form of love but rather essential for one's ability to give and receive love from others. Without loving and respecting oneself, it becomes difficult to extend the same to others.

Having explored the various types of love—eros, ludus, storge, philia, mania, pragma, agape, and philautia—let us now delve into the concept of the most ideal form of love, endless love.

## Endless Love

Endless love encompasses enduring patience within the three components of love: intimacy, involvement, and passion. The epitome of patient love can be found in the biblical passage below:

"Love is patient and kind; love does not envy or boast; it is not arrogant or rude. It does not insist on its own way; it is not irritable or resentful; it does not rejoice at wrongdoing, but rejoices with the truth. Love bears all things, believes all things, hopes all things, endures all things." (Corinthians 13:4-7)

Love in the Bible is gentle, devoid of envy, bragging, arrogance, or rudeness. It remains composed and does not harbor thoughts of evil or injustice. True love rejoices in the truth, embraces belief, sustains hope, and endures all things. The key to endless love lies in its ability to be patient and endure everything for the sake of the other person.

Endless love is about emulating God's deep, high, wide, and long love. To achieve an endless love with our beloved, we must continuously cultivate patience and endurance for one another. However, the endless love of parents for their children comes naturally and instinctively, requiring no training.

Among the many examples of endless love, let's consider the story of a couple who have sustained their love throughout the passage of time, proving its endless love.

From the moment they first met, they developed a mutual attraction and exchanged warm smiles. As they started dating, their love blossomed. They pledged to stand shoulder to shoulder, achieving countless dreams and goals together. Through trust and perseverance, they awaited the fulfillment of their aspirations. However, life presented unexpected challenges, including financial difficulties, health issues, and conflicts with those around them. Each day became a heavy burden, and their future appeared uncertain.

Nevertheless, their love provided them with an unknown strength and a profound connection that supported one another during these trying times. They refused to give up on their dreams and goals, demonstrating patience and endurance for each other. This mutual trust and love were vital in weathering the storms of life. Despite facing hardships and heartaches, they continuously supported and encouraged one another. Instead of sacrificing themselves, they chose to uplift and grow stronger together. They have overcome life's adversities in a unique way, maintained a stable family, and their children have grown up well. Through perseverance, they emerged stronger from tough times, and their love deepened even further.

Their unwavering trust and understanding brought them closer, and their love provided new strength and enthusiasm. Their shared motto, "The essence of love is to be patient and endure everything," fueled their endless love. As time passed, wrinkles appeared on their faces and the backs of their hands, but their love for each other deepened, bringing them much happiness.

Endless love is a love that lasts even for a lifetime, shining like a lamp that never wavers in the darkest of times. It brings boundless joy, peace, comfort, and happiness to each other's lives, and so much more. Amidst long waits and enduring patience, life blossoms into a beautiful flower with endless love. May our future shine until the end and be blessed with infinite love.

I hope our love overflows like a river, healing painful wounds, restoring broken relationships, and deepening the beauty of our love, leading to greater happiness.

# 10.
# Grow with an Open Heart

While our bodies may cease to physically grow, our minds possess an infinite capacity for growth. The mind encompasses an individual's personality, emotions, will, and introspection. It perceives, thinks, reasons, judges, and serves as a means of self-control. The broadest and most open mind can embrace even the vastness of the universe. As we expand the breadth and openness of our minds, the quality and happiness of our lives undergo profound changes.

Quoting Longfellow's famous poem "A Psalm of Life," let us contrast those with closed minds and those with open minds. People who say, "Life is but an empty dream," live with closed minds. In contrast, those who proclaim, "Life is real! Life is earnest!" and strive for tomorrow more than today, lead noble lives with open minds and a relentless pursuit of achievement.

To foster the growth of our minds, large and open, we must fortify our inner resilience and mental muscles. American psychotherapist and healing counselor Noelle Nelson shares six mental habits that nurture inner strength:

1. Believe in your life energy: Recognize your inherent vitality. You possess remarkable life energy; employ it wisely, engaging in new hobbies, exercise, or novel pursuits.
2. Don't linger on others' criticisms: Critique holds a dual nature. Embrace it as an opportunity for self-reflection.
3. Release perfectionism: Perfectionism can be detrimental; life evolves, and imperfections are natural.
4. Rise after each fall: When you stumble, acknowledge your emotions and regain composure resolutely.
5. Walk through anger: Anger impairs rationality and focus. A 20-minute walk outdoors can restore equilibrium.
6. Awaken your inner hero: Within us lies an innate potential for compassion, courage, and care. Nurture this inner hero.

When fortified with inner resilience, we can cultivate an open mind. Life's contentment parallels the expansiveness of one's mind.

An open-minded and continuously growing individual is someone who:
- Engages in self-reflection when faced with adversity.
- Possesses the willingness to learn amidst challenges.

- Demonstrates self-objectivity and accurately assesses their current state.
- Displays a strong sense of purpose, prioritizing the community over individual interests.
- Puts effort into continuous self-improvement and dedication.

Encouraging open-minded experiences in individuals reduces the likelihood of developing mental health issues, including depression, panic disorders, obsessive-compulsive disorder, schizophrenia, and anxiety disorders.

In conclusion, to cultivate an open mind, you must fortify your inner resilience and embrace the following principles:

1. Foster a positive mindset to live joyfully and gratefully, and embrace challenges with courage, free from fear of failure.
2. Demonstrate humility, consideration for others, and effective self-care. Find happiness in the journey rather than fixating solely on outcomes.
3. Be a conduit of blessings, allowing love to flow through you. Maintain a gentle smile and positive demeanor.
4. Practice patience and emotional control, particularly during disagreements. A 6-second pause allows for rational decision-making as information travels from the cerebrum to the cerebral cortex. Swiftly forgive past hurts and painful memories for enduring happiness.

5. Choose a role model from history, the Bible, or contemporary figures. Strive to emulate them and expand the boundaries of your mind endlessly.

Open-minded individuals approach each day with positivity, becoming sources of happiness and positivity themselves.

They prioritize self-care to create a conducive environment for personal development. This mindset involves nurturing a broad perspective, spreading positivity, making a positive impact, aspiring for the future, and leading a fulfilling life filled with hope.

# 11.
# How to Improve Your Memory

The brain is a complex organ composed of nerve cells that form a central nervous system, controlling various aspects of an animal's behavior and functioning. It regulates movements, behaviors, and vital functions such as heartbeat, blood pressure, and body temperature. Additionally, the brain handles cognition, emotions, and learning processes. Short-term memory involves the temporary storage of information through neurotransmitter release in nerve cell circuits. Transitioning from short-term to long-term memory involves the activation of new neural networks, creating lasting circuits among nerve cells.

Long-term memory develops over time and encompasses memories, knowledge, and experiences that contribute to an individual's identity. However, not all memories become long-term; the brain filters out unnecessary details, retaining only essential information.

Three Strategies to Enhance Memory
1. Draw from Personal Experiences: Using your own real experiences helps encode memories effectively.
2. Employ Strong Introductions: Providing a robust introduction to new information enhances its retention.
3. Create Associative Environments: Environments that trigger memories contribute to better encoding and recall.

Ten Brain Exercises for an 80% Memory Boost
1. Read Aloud: Reading aloud reinforces memory by engaging both speaking and listening processes.
2. Hand Alternation: Using hands alternately in daily tasks sharpens brain function and memory.
3. Aerobic Exercise: Increasing heart rate through regular aerobic exercise boosts long-term memory.
4. Chopstick Use: Using chopsticks stimulates cell projections and nerve cell expansion.
5. Word Associations: Engaging in word associations and endings keeps the brain active and sharp.
6. Observe Four Traits: Choose one person you encounter daily, observe them closely, and focus on identifying four traits to enhance memory recall.

7. Music Enrichment: Listening to lyric-free music aids information retention.
8. Fist Clenching: Clenching fists for 90 seconds aids memory formation.
9. Doodling: Doodling prevents distraction and improves information recall.
10. Laughter: Laughing reduces cortisol levels linked to aging and disease, benefitting memory.

Remember, even as adults, the brain continues to develop. Since memory plays a significant role in our lives, applying these strategies and exercises can lead to continuous improvement.

# 12.
# How to Manage Your Anger

Anger is a harmful human emotion, defined as a negative emotional state that arises when one's desires are obstructed or when forced to do something. It can manifest in various unreasonable situations, such as infringement of interests, forced suffering, threats, and more.

Most individuals harbor some resentment due to conflicts in relationships and unfair treatment. Anger is often triggered by stress, failure, injustice, or helplessness. Uncontrolled anger can lead to issues in relationships, work, and overall quality of life, causing impulsive actions that harm oneself and others.

Anger involves both psychological and physiological elements, driven by brain chemicals. The amygdala in the brain's cerebellum triggers emotional responses, leading to a cascade of reactions, including the release of adrenaline. This can result in a heightened heart rate and readiness to respond to threats.

To manage anger effectively:
1. Take Breaks: When feeling angry, step away, take a deep breath, and distance yourself from the source of anger to calm your mind.
2. Count Slowly: Count from 1 to 10 slowly while focusing on deep breathing, allowing time to relax and calm down.
3. Change Responses: Avoid being overwhelmed by anger; practice self-control through methods like meditation, yoga, deep breathing, or exercise.
4. Express Calmly: After cooling down, assess the situation and assert your opinion calmly and rationally.
5. Think Before Speaking: Take a moment to organize your thoughts before engaging in a conversation to avoid regrettable words.
6. Be Specific and Respectful: Express dissatisfaction with respect and specificity to address grievances more effectively.
7. Seek Solutions: Analyze the cause of anger and focus on finding solutions. Self-reflection is crucial in understanding both sides of the situation.
8. Meditate and Exercise: Regular meditation and aerobic exercise help stabilize the mind, reduce stress, and alleviate anger.
9. Self-Reflection: Look in the mirror to observe your angry expression and gain insight into how others perceive you.

10. Seek Help: If managing anger becomes challenging, consider consulting professionals like neuropsychiatrists or anger management counselors for guidance and possible treatment.

By mastering anger control, interpersonal relationships improve, personalities mature, and overall well-being enhances, leading to a more positive and stable life.

# Section Three:
## The Eyes are The Lamp of The Heart

# 13.
# Tapping into Good Habits

Judgment is the conscious aspect of our mind, while habit resides in the unconscious. Habits are automatic actions performed by the unconscious mind when specific conditions are met. When a conscious action consistently produces positive results upon encountering a specific signal, the brain stores it in the realm of the unconscious. As a result, judgmental work by the conscious mind is no longer necessary. These stored actions in the unconscious realm are referred to as habits. The unconscious mind operates swiftly and accurately, and these habits can also influence other aspects of our lives.

The cultivation of good habits holds significant importance in our lives, as they have a profound impact on us. Just like the proverbial saying, "Habits formed at an early age persist until old age," habits not only shape our character deep within our consciousness but also serve as a crucial benchmark for determining whether we lead a meaningful life.

Life demands certain principles, and acquiring the wisdom to govern our own lives is crucial. Acting in accordance with principles yields positive outcomes, while deviating from them results in negative consequences. When we make a promise to someone and honor that commitment, we earn their trust. Moreover, adhering to the right principles can provide the impetus to effectively achieve our life goals.

Expanding the realm of positive thoughts is also essential. To broaden the scope of our thoughts, we need to exercise our imagination by envisioning in detail the meaning of life bestowed upon us. Dr. Einstein (1879-1955) once said, "Imagination is more important than knowledge. Knowledge is limited, but imagination encircles the world." Imagination enables us to envision possibilities, discover untapped potential, reveal the unseen, and create something out of nothing. It is the foundation for dreams, aspirations, and ideals to flourish. Setting life goals, visualizing and experiencing the desired outcomes beforehand are all acts of imagination. When faced with hardships and paralyzed by the fear of failure, it is through imagination that we can summon the wisdom to overcome these obstacles.

Additionally, incorporating the habit of reading the Bible, engaging with good literature, or listening to inspiring words is essential. These practices allow us to gain wisdom, find inner peace, nurture a vibrant imagination, and draw inspiration to invigorate our souls, thereby cultivating the habit of enriching our lives.

There exist numerous effective ways to lead a fulfilling life, and one of them is engraving our purpose and principles into our hearts, as well as documenting them. This method helps solidify these principles and goals within our subconscious, leading to the formation of habits. Consequently, this becomes a driving force for creativity, as it organizes and concretizes our thoughts.

Good habits permeate our body and mind through consistent repetition. They manifest in various ways, such as leading a disciplined life, maintaining a courteous demeanor, fostering positive thinking, embracing diligence and sincerity, cultivating an open mind, pursuing lifelong learning, engaging in meditation, reading books, and practicing love and kindness towards our fellow human beings.

Stephen Covey (1932-2012), a renowned management consultant, emphasized the following principles in his book 'The 7 Habits of Highly Effective People.'

Firstly, take charge of your own life.

Secondly, when approaching work, begin with the end goal in mind.

Thirdly, prioritize and focus on important matters first.

Fourthly, seek mutual benefit and consideration rather than self-interest.

Fifthly, when persuading others, seek to understand them before seeking to be understood.

Sixthly, strive for synergistic outcomes, achieving more than the sum of individual efforts.

Seventhly, continually renew oneself, among other habits.

These habits, which guide individual lives and collective destinies toward success, greatly assist in realizing one's true nature, the significance of one's life, and one's unique abilities. Throughout the process of discovering the true value of life, these habits support self-identity, sincerity, self-control, and originality. By adopting these habits, one can heal and rebuild deteriorated or broken human relationships and transform existing positive relationships into even more fulfilling ones. This holds the secret to experiencing deeper intimacy, enhanced creativity, and progressive personal growth.

The habit of constant renewal pertains to the practice of recharging oneself. It is an essential quality that transitions from a dependent stage, where others are the subjects, to an independent stage, where the self becomes the subject. These virtues embody an ideal human image in which the self takes the lead, fostering reciprocal development among all members of society.

Good habits are cultivated through conscious training and repetition. Whether consciously or unconsciously, habits shape our character through training and are reflected in our actions, ultimately determining the trajectory of our lives. The quality of our habits plays a crucial role in living a prosperous life.

# 14.
# Tearing Down the Tower of Babel Within Us

The story of the Tower of Babel in the Bible delivers a powerful message for us today. Humanity has always lived selfishly, and the sin of fallen humanity has led to betrayal and estrangement from God. Their ambition was not only to build a tower that reached the heavens but also to let their pride rise to the skies. This behavior is still evident in the lives of modern people.

Just as uncut hair grows and becomes difficult to manage, unchecked desire grows and becomes harder to control. Thousands of years ago, when God grew weary of humanity's endless sinfulness, He chose the righteous man Noah and commanded him to prepare for a great flood. This flood would destroy all humanity, and God planned to repopulate the earth through Noah's descendants. However, humanity again strayed from God's will. "Come, let us build ourselves a city and a tower with its top in the heavens, and let us make a name for ourselves, lest we be dispersed over the face of the whole earth." (Genesis 11 : 4)

Only after God scattered them across the earth and confused their language did they stop building the Tower of Babel. The Bible is filled with stories of people deliberately defying God's will and succumbing to their selfish, sinful nature. When we ignore God and choose to follow our own path, we inevitably fall into negative emotions like arrogance, bitterness, and vengeance. We must be cautious. When we first disobey God, we start laying the foundation of the Tower of Babel in our hearts.

Once the first brick is laid, laying the next one becomes easier, and the next one even easier. Eventually, often without realizing it, we build a tower that reaches the heavens, symbolizing our perceived equality with God.

The roots of Western culture lie in ancient Greece and Rome, which worshipped multiple gods. These polytheistic religions revered various gods, with the twelve most important deities believed to reside on Mount Olympus, Greece's highest peak. The Greeks attributed human emotions and physical traits to their gods, though only the gods were considered eternal. Greek mythology formed the foundation of Western literature and visual arts.

A prevalent theme in ancient Greek literature is revenge. For example, one of the most famous works in literary history is Homer's Iliad (circa 800 BC). Key figures like Achilles,

Agamemnon, and Hector are all obsessed with avenging themselves on their enemies. One act of revenge begets another, leading to an endless cycle of violence.

Other great literary works from ancient Greece follow this pattern. Homer's Odyssey, Aeschylus's Oresteia trilogy, Sophocles's Ajax, and Euripides's Medea and Orestes are all examples.

From God's perspective, we were created in His image, but our sin separates us from Him. This terrible gap could only be bridged through the sacrifice of Jesus Christ. In Shakespeare's Hamlet (1601), the Prince of Denmark contemplates whether to end his life or not, famously declaring, "To be, or not to be, that is the question." Yet, our existence and death are determined not by our choice but by God's will. When we do not place God at the center of our lives, we essentially choose to live for ourselves first, leading to ruin. Separation from God is ruin.

Fyodor Dostoevsky's Crime and Punishment (1866) and The Brothers Karamazov (1879-80), Stendhal's The Red and the Black (1830), Alexandre Dumas's The Count of Monte Cristo (1844-46), and Theodore Dreiser's An American Tragedy(1925) are all excellent books, but they share a common theme: they all honestly depict the universality of human sinfulness. These works suggest that despite modern society's technological, scientific, and material advancements, humanity has disregarded God and placed itself at the center of the universe.

Despite all we have built, we have destroyed much. Ethics and morality have collapsed, and chaos reigns. We have disobeyed God and built the Tower of Babel in our hearts. Pursuing our dreams and ideals without God is ultimately meaningless. As another of Shakespeare's great tragic characters, Macbeth, laments, it is "a tale told by an idiot, full of sound and fury, signifying nothing."

Another common theme in many great literary works is the search for utopia, an ideal perfect place. Thomas More's Utopia (1516), Tommaso Campanella's The City of the Sun (1602), Francis Bacon's New Atlantis (1627), Daniel Defoe's Robinson Crusoe (1719), Jonathan Swift's Gulliver's Travels (1726), and Edward Bellamy's Looking Backward (1888) are examples of such works. Of course, utopia does not exist in this world. Even if humans could design and build a utopia, disregarding our sinful nature, it would never be more than a Tower of Babel.

Unless God is the foundation, everything we build will inevitably crumble. "Unless the Lord builds the house, those who build it labor in vain. Unless the Lord watches over the city, the watchman stays awake in vain." (Psalms 127 : 1)

If we do not base our lives on God's word, our sinful nature will eventually build the Tower of Babel in our hearts. This tower is not made of bricks and mortar but of negative emotions like envy, resentment, distrust, greed, and pride. These emotions arise when we intentionally distance ourselves from our Creator.

It is a constant struggle, but if we live daily according to God's word, we can tear down the Tower of Babel forming in our hearts. This is how we receive new life from the Lord and give new life to others.

# 15.
# Always Be Grateful

As we go through life, we often use the phrases "thank you" and "thanks." There are so many things in the world to be grateful for. Living a life of gratitude makes life happier, transforms our personality to be more optimistic, and leads to a more energetic life. Additionally, it helps us engage passionately in activities, develop a sense of humor, be perceived as generous and kind by others, and view situations with a more creative and open perspective.

When we cultivate a grateful heart, the left prefrontal cortex of the brain becomes activated, leading to positive emotions. Furthermore, it activates parts of the brain related to forming social connections, giving us a sense of security and trust in our relationships with others. Gratitude also impacts the body by reducing stress, stabilizing heart rate and blood pressure, relaxing muscles, reducing inflammation, and boosting immunity. It releases happiness hormones such as dopamine, serotonin, and endorphins, which improve the quality of our sleep and optimize the functions of our brain and body.

A person who is grateful for even the smallest things is a happy person. God blesses those with a grateful heart with joy, peace, and happiness. On the other hand, a life without gratitude towards God brings anxiety, fear, and dissatisfaction. The peace and satisfaction that come from a grateful heart are well expressed by the 19th-century French writer Alphonse Karr:

"Some people grumble that roses have thorns; I am grateful that thorns have roses." — Alphonse Karr (1808-1890)

Our perspective on life is determined by whether we have a grateful heart or a discontented heart. When we give thanks to God, His peaceful and loving presence becomes strongly evident in our lives.

Nicolas Herman (1611-1691), also known as Brother Lawrence, was a French monk who understood the importance of living in God's presence through everyday conversation with Him. While working in the monastery kitchen for 15 years, he felt God's presence even during the most mundane tasks like washing dishes or cooking eggs. After his death, his letters and conversations were published in the book "The Practice of the Presence of God," where he explained simple ways to live in God's presence in our daily lives.

As many who have lived monastic lives attest, one sure way to experience God's presence is through simple household chores. Brother Lawrence approached all mundane tasks with a heart of true love and obedience, always striving to offer pure love and devotion to God. Following Brother Lawrence's example, if we approach our everyday tasks with joy, we will discover that God's presence is not only evident in the infinite stars shining in the night sky, the vast seas covering the earth, or the majestic mountains rising above, but also in the smallest things and quietest corners of our lives. Be grateful to God for the little things. By doing so, you will live in His presence.

If we can value the most ordinary tasks God has given us and cherish everyone we meet as God's children, our anxieties and complaints will disappear, replaced by a grateful heart. Dietrich Bonhoeffer (1906-1945), a German theologian executed by the Nazis for his involvement in a plot to assassinate Hitler, expressed his gratitude for maintaining friendships even while imprisoned. In his collection of writings from prison, "Letters and Papers from Prison," Bonhoeffer shared how thankful he was for these visits:

"You see, it would be wrong to suppose that prison life is uninterrupted torture, It certainly is not, and visits like yours relieve it for days on end, even though they do, of course, awaken feelings that have fortunately lain dormant for a while. But that does not matter either. I realize again in thankfulness how well off I was, and feel new hope and energy. Thank you very much, you yourself and the others..."

There are countless things in our lives to be thankful to God for, and giving thanks to God means acknowledging that our existence is not by chance. Furthermore, it deepens our understanding that we are God's children. Even though we cannot predict the future, if we strive to walk with God daily, the burden of our anxieties and worries will be lightened because God shares them with us. People who live life complaining and not thanking God will eventually lose all perspective. They will place themselves before God and be consumed by dissatisfaction. Excessive complaining and worrying can have negative psychological and physical effects. Anxiety spreads throughout our existence like a virus, accompanied by related symptoms such as fear, doubt, frustration, irritation, jealousy, greed, and depression.

"A joyful heart is good medicine, but a crushed spirit dries up the bones."(Proverbs 17 : 22)

It is foolish to worry about tomorrow if we cannot take care of today. Faith helps us manage our problems and view them with the right perspective.

Let us praise the Lord who came to this earth for our salvation. Let us thank the Lord who strengthens us when we are weak. Let us praise the Lord who is always with us when we are downhearted, joyful, in physical or emotional pain, and even when performing the smallest tasks. Let us thank the Lord who has given us eternal life. Let us confess that the only thing we can offer to the Lord is our gratitude.

# 16.
# Humbling Oneself Under God's Mighty Hand

God bestows grace upon the humble. When we humble ourselves under His mighty hand, God blesses our entire lives. Because our eternal future lies under His powerful hand, we must lower ourselves even more. No matter how much we strive for perfection, in this imperfect world, we always feel a sense of lack. Our ultimate destination is eternal life with our Father in heaven. Yet, we often act as if we will live forever in this world, turning our backs on God with pride and shortsightedness. Human nature seeks personal happiness first, leading to the arrogant belief that everything we possess is ours, even those things that are not. Only when we humble ourselves before God do we learn the meaning of a fruitful life. Such humility before God is the only way to live wisely.

By following God's Word and practicing His teachings, we can learn true humility. The Bible emphasizes the importance of humility, and Jesus demonstrated it through His life. Though He was the Son of God, He came in the form of a lowly servant to serve and love. By following Jesus' example, we can understand the true meaning of humility.

Moreover, through humility, we can experience great grace in our relationships with others. When we respect and consider others with a humble heart, we can build deeper and more meaningful relationships. God commands us to love and serve one another, and through this, we can convey God's love to the world.

Therefore, humility before God is not only crucial in our relationship with Him but also a vital virtue in our daily lives. We must rely on God daily, seek His wisdom, and practice humility in all our actions and thoughts. By living this way, God will bless us and reveal His glory through us.

I learn the wisdom of humility whenever I listen to Schubert's "Unfinished Symphony." At the age of 25, Schubert composed Symphony No. 8 in B minor, known as the "Unfinished Symphony." Typically, symphonies are composed of four movements, but the "Unfinished Symphony" includes only two. Despite its incomplete form, Schubert's "Unfinished Symphony" has been loved by music enthusiasts worldwide as much as Beethoven's Symphony No. 5 "Fate", Tchaikovsky's Symphony No. 6 "Pathétique," and Berlioz's "Symphonie fantastique."

Schubert was one of the greatest composers of the Romantic era. His "Unfinished Symphony" is beautiful and rich in melody, and his use of harmony is excellent. Often, while listening to this symphony, I wonder why it is so highly praised by musicians and critics despite being shorter than most symphonies. Is it because the content is complete despite its form being incomplete? Or is there an inherent beauty in the very nature of its incompleteness? Perhaps the melody of this piece leaves a deep impression on us, like a mysterious tune softly carried to our ears by the wind.

As I am not a professional musician or music critic, it is challenging to understand in musical terms why the "Unfinished Symphony" is so highly regarded. However, every time I listen to this piece, I am reminded that no matter how long we live on this earth, life remains unfinished. We can find completion only in heaven with God. Life on earth is like a journey, and soon, we must return to our Father's house in heaven. When we are young, we feel as if we will live forever, but as we grow older, we become more aware of the passage of time and realize how short life is. The horizon seems distant, but we fill the empty spaces of life with various activities to avoid thinking about the inevitability of death. Yet, no matter how hard we try to fill those spaces, we can never fully fill them. Death makes us honest, and some people, when faced with death, strongly feel the incompleteness of life with regret.

I often felt that something was missing in my life. Sometimes I feel a void, which is why I enjoy listening to Schubert's "Unfinished Symphony." And although my opinion may differ from that of professional musicians or critics, I believe the power of the "Unfinished Symphony" comes from its incompleteness. Schubert's symphony reminds us of our inadequacies. This mysterious power common to all great works of art acts as a mirror reflecting our shortcomings, and in front of it, we become humble.

We have an endless desire to be noticed. It is in our nature to want to be favorably evaluated by others. But Schubert's "Unfinished Symphony" teaches us how to control this desire. Wisdom lies in acknowledging our imperfections. Our earthly life is inherently incomplete, and therefore we must live humbly. To maintain humility, we must be wary of flattery and personal recognition, which strongly stimulate our desire to be known to others. If we are not cautious and do not train ourselves in humility, the desire for recognition will incite our vanity. That vanity constantly tempts us just below the surface.

At the same time, we know notable public figures who are excellent examples of humility. One of them is former U.S. President Jimmy Carter, who has long been involved in charity work through Habitat for Humanity. Another is Albert Schweitzer (1875-1965), who, as a musician, theologian, and doctor, devoted much of his life to helping the poor in Gabon, West Africa. And there is Mother Teresa (1910-1997), who dedicated her life to serving the poor and marginalized in Kolkata, India. These three people followed the example of the Son of God, who came to this earth to serve the weak, the poor, and the marginalized. Why did Christ give up the glory of heaven and come to this earth as a servant, humbling Himself to the point of dying on the cross? Because God exalts those who humbly serve others.

# 17.
# The Eyes Are the Lamp of the Heart

There are the physical eyes, the eyes of the heart, the eyes of wisdom, and the spiritual eyes. In the physical world, our physical eyes receive light and enable us to distinguish objects. The more light we have, the clearer our perception becomes, and darkness hinders our ability to see clearly.

To live beautifully in this world, we must open the eyes of our hearts and look at the world. When watching a sunset, some people feel hope for tomorrow, while others feel sadness. The eyes of our hearts determine our happiness. We see the world through the windows of our hearts, and we can accept it with joy and pain. We have the right and duty to choose a satisfying life. Through various states of heart, we discover how to love life.

If the eyes of our hearts are closed, the eyes through which we see the world become gloomy and our hearts darken, but when our hearts are open, there is joy, gratitude, and hope. An open heart invites light. Expanding the windows of our hearts opens new horizons. Beyond the windows of our hearts, there is energy and mystery. As our inner light shines, we can discover our own stories and dreams. A person whose inner light shines loves and forgives even in difficult times and lives romantically and humbly. Living romantically means accepting each day as if it were the last and striving to do our best. Medieval monks greeted the morning with the contemplation of death, 'Memento Mori' ('Remember you must die'), to cultivate humility and reflection on life.

Beyond the eyes of the heart, there are the spiritual eyes. Just as the physical eyes need light to see, our spiritual eyes also need light to recognize truth and avoid falling into darkness. Jesus compared the eyes to the lamp of the body. "The eye is the lamp of the body. So if your eye is healthy, your whole body will be full of light; but if your eye is unhealthy, your whole body will be full of darkness." Through His teachings, we understand that the state of our spiritual eyes reflects the state of our hearts. Healthy eyes symbolize a heart full of goodness and truth, making judgments and intentions clear and righteous. Conversely, unhealthy spiritual eyes result in darkness permeating the person's entire being.

The core of this metaphor goes beyond simple physical sight to delve into the realm of discernment and perception. Through insight, individuals can see beyond superficial appearances and grasp deeper truths of the universe. True spiritual wisdom, rooted in the understanding of divine truth, represents healthy spiritual eyes. Through this wisdom, individuals can accurately perceive spiritual realities and recognize the existence of higher authority and eternal kingdoms. To fulfill God's plan and comprehend the mysteries of the spiritual realm, it is essential to keep our spiritual eyes open and receptive. Many people long to glimpse the mysterious world through awakened spiritual sight and recognize the inherent beauty veiled by darkness. Through continuous spiritual growth and enlightenment, we can illuminate the true light of divine knowledge and behold the beauty of God's creation with clarity and reverence.

# 18.
# For the Lonely Soul

In this world, there are people who experience happiness, relaxation, gratitude, and confidence, while others feel lonely, alienated, depressed, and critical. Some individuals even go as far as ending their own lives due to the immense suffering they endure. The Bible teaches us that a single life holds more value than the entire world combined.

Lonely souls can become our family and neighbors.

If we truly love our families and neighbors, we must take an active interest in their lives, whether at home, at work, or at social gatherings. When they feel lonely and seek conversation, it is important that we listen to them so that they can share their concerns. During these conversations, we can also lead discussions on matters of spiritual salvation. Often people who live alone try to find solutions to their problems on their own. As a result, their hearts are hardened and they struggle to accept God's love and become sad beings. Until we recognize that we are human beings who have come to live in remembrance of God, we must open our ears, listen, listen, and give comfort and comfort.

Blaise Pascal (1623-1662), a prominent French Christian thinker, skillfully dealt with human contradictions and instability in his posthumous work, Pensées (1670). Pascal argues

"It is futile to seek within oneself the solution to all one's unhappiness. As one's knowledge grows, the realization arises that neither truth nor goodness can be found only within. Philosophers have not found the cause of the solution to unhappiness, despite their promise that it can be found."

Pascal argues that philosophers are doomed to misfortune because they do not know what constitutes their true state and ultimate good. He identifies pride as the greatest affliction that plagues philosophers, leading them away from God and enslaving them to worldly problems. Even if philosophers make God the object of study, it only boosts their ego. When individuals are alienated from God, they inevitably fall into a state of loneliness and desolation. No matter how diligently you work towards your ambitions and how much time, talents, effort, and resources you devote, you miss the purpose in life.

Whether people are happy, sad, lonely, or content, companionship is essential for a fulfilling life. When plagued by physical ailments, emotional distress, heartbreak, or the pain of separation, individuals long for someone to lean on, seeking courage and yearning to restore love and hope.

There is a great deal of suffering in the world—much of it. There is suffering caused by hunger, homelessness, and various diseases. However, I firmly believe that the most profound suffering comes from the feeling of loneliness, the sense of being unloved, and the experience of having no one. I have increasingly come to understand that being unwanted is the most devastating affliction any human being

The passage above is a paraphrase of a segment from Mother Teresa's (1919-97) "Warm Hands." It suggests that the most excruciating pain in the world is the feeling of isolation, the absence of love, and the belief that no one is there for me. Humans are not meant to live solely focused on themselves; instead, we are meant to live in harmony with others, and our existence is sustained through love. What we can offer to those who are marginalized and suffering is our compassion, love, and warm hearts.

Assisting our neighbors who are in despair and suffering, on the verge of giving up due to depression and anguish, and helping them emerge from the darkness to embrace hope, is a precious and invaluable endeavor. We accomplish this by extending our warm hearts and love. When we save the souls of others, our own souls also flourish and grow stronger, thriving in all aspects of life.

Those who guide numerous individuals toward righteousness will shine like eternal stars in the sky. Similarly, like a tree planted beside flowing streams of water that bears fruit in its appointed season without withering leaves, they will be blessed and prosper in their circumstances and life.

# Section Four:
## The Power of Gratitude

# 19.
# Relationship between Science and Faith

The advancement of science and technology has significantly contributed to the progress of human civilization. We currently reside in an era dominated by scientific civilization, witnessing continuous developments in modern science. This rapid progression encompasses new revelations about the origins of the universe and the mysteries surrounding life. Fields like genetic engineering have made substantial contributions to food production, while biotechnology has enabled us to conquer nearly all human diseases and extend life expectancy. Science and technology continue to thrive in various domains, including communication, big data, automobile technology, home appliances, e-books, electronic voting, computer utilization, nuclear power technology, and artificial intelligence.

As our civilization advances, we should appreciate the wisdom bestowed upon us by God and draw closer to Him. Unfortunately, it appears that the world is moving in a different direction. Regardless of the extent of human scientific achievements, they are ultimately insignificant in the grand context of God's history.

Reflecting on the development of scientific civilization and contemplating the significance of faith allows us to introspect as human beings while contemplating our relationship with God. The Book of Job delivers a poignant message, challenging human arrogance and reminding us of our insignificance: "who is this that darkens my counsel with words without knowledge? Brace yourself like a man: I will question you, and you shall answer me. Where were you when I laid the earth's foundation? Tell me, if you understand." (Job 38:2-4)

Although today's scientific civilization appears to gradually uncover the universe's secrets, the words of Job remind us that we have only scratched the surface. No matter how hard humans strive, we can never fully comprehend the workings of celestial bodies, the secrets of light, or the intricate order of the vast sky. These matters fall under the unique authority of God, the absolute sovereign.

In ancient times, Aristotle, a Greek philosopher hailed as the father of learning, postulated that heavier objects fell faster than lighter ones. However, after 2,000 years, Galileo of Italy refuted this theory. Through the free fall experiment conducted at the Leaning Tower of Pisa, he demonstrated that objects fall at the same speed regardless of their weight.

During Copernicus' time in Poland, the prevalent belief was in the geocentric theory, asserting that the sun and the moon revolved around the Earth—a notion the church acknowledged. However, Copernicus delved into astronomy and presented a thesis titled "On the Rotation of Celestial Bodies," arguing for the heliocentric theory that the Earth revolves around the sun. Galileo of Italy and Kepler of Germany subsequently supported and substantiated his claims.

Though it may be challenging to accept, the progress of science has been gradual. Science exists within the wisdom of God, the creator of the heavens and the Earth. Each time human knowledge encounters its limits, we should not attribute it solely to our own abilities. Perhaps God's mysterious providence is restricting our access.

In just 500 years, science has undergone rapid development, persisting at an unprecedented pace. We currently reside in an advanced civilization, where machines can even perceive human warmth. Auto-sensing systems open doors automatically upon approach, and water flows from faucets upon a hand's proximity. When entering a house or apartment at night, the ceiling light by the front door illuminates automatically. Many of the automatic sensing technologies we employ today are based on invisible infrared light. Although emitted in minute quantities, even warm-blooded creatures such as humans emit infrared rays corresponding to body temperature. Automatic detectors, or sensors, find wide applications in unmanned detection devices, remote controls, and guided missiles. Robots have emerged to perform tasks that humans find challenging, such as cleaning houses, assembling cars, and exploring the depths of the ocean. Moreover, modern science and technology, encompassing nuclear weapons, life cloning, genetic manipulation, computers, and cyberspace, continue to advance.

However advanced science becomes, it merely allows us to gradually uncover God's mysterious providence through human knowledge.

In the present era, the Internet's development has facilitated global email communication and granted access to vast amounts of data and information, as exemplified by ChatGPT. Artificial intelligence (AI) technology is transforming society, from chatbots to autonomous vehicles, as it becomes increasingly widespread. With advancements in AI technology, automation in manufacturing and service industries is expected to enhance productivity and operational efficiency. Nonetheless, profound contemplation is necessary. As modern scientific civilization progresses and our lives become more comfortable, there is a risk of our mental and spiritual worlds growing complacent and lazy, distancing us from God. During such times, it is crucial to remain vigilant, renew our souls, and live according to the Word.

Believing only in what we see, confirm, and comprehend is an arrogant act that prioritizes human knowledge. It is akin to attempting to snatch sovereignty from God's hands and create human laws. Faith transcends mere navigational skills, enabling us to navigate through treacherous waves and avoid reefs while sailing. It resembles the trust placed in an experienced captain who can perceive the invisible, like an underwater rock or an unexpected current. This is why we must rely on the invisible power of God and live in "trust in the invisible God." If we live solely by human knowledge—fleshly faith—our spirits are destined to wither away. We must embrace the wisdom and Word of God to open our spirits and experience life and peace.

Regardless of the advancements in science, we must live within God's wisdom. As the history of science demonstrates, the knowledge amassed by humans pales in comparison to the vastness of God's wisdom, akin to trivial grains of sand scattered on the seashore.

Living according to the flesh erects barriers between our spirits and God. Yet, if we embrace God's wisdom and Word, our spirits will naturally open, allowing us to enjoy life and find peace. Hence, in this modern era, it is essential to contemplate the intricate relationship between the development of scientific civilization and faith. No matter how much science progresses, we must live within God's wisdom.

# 20.
# Overcoming Trials

As we live our lives, we inevitably encounter trials and tribulations. These trials, large and small, crash upon the shores of our lives like waves. From personal trials like loneliness, loss, failure, and illness to societal trials like injustice and absurdity, how can we overcome these challenges? Continuing to think amidst hardship and adversity grants us growth and a keen insight into the world.

Often, trials and tribulations are caused by those close to us, such as colleagues, friends, and family. They may be calculated to harm us, like rumors, or may result from arbitrary situations like losing a job or the death of a loved one. Our desires and aspirations can also test us. Regardless of the type of trial we face, do not consider it meaningless suffering.

"When one door closes, another opens. But often, we look so regretfully at the closed door that we fail to see the one that has opened for us." — Alexander Graham Bell (1847-1922), Inventor of the Telephone

God allows trials for our maturity, meaning every trial is an opportunity for spiritual growth. Through trials, we learn valuable lessons. For example, we learn honesty by overcoming deceit, humility by overcoming pride, and perseverance by overcoming the desire to give up when faced with challenges. Success is born from adversity.

Trials also bring additional temptations. Let's examine the four stages of how Satan tempts us.

First, Satan plants seeds of desire in our hearts. If we do not make a conscious effort to remove them, these desires grow quietly like weeds and choke our virtues. Beware of easy shortcuts, for they may be Satan's temptations.

The second stage is doubt. Satan makes us doubt what God's word says about sin. He plants negative thoughts and emotions like jealousy and pride, causing us to feel anxiety and doubt about the things God has given us.

The third stage is deception. Satan whispers lies in our ears, making them seem as if they come from God. For example, even though we know the importance of honesty, we may falsely believe that being honest in a particular situation would cause more harm.

The fourth stage is disobedience. Through Satan's deception, our thoughts deviate from God's will, leading us to disobey Him and fall into Satan's traps.

When we succumb to temptation and fall into Satan's trap, we may experience temporary pleasure and joy. However, that pleasure and joy soon turn into pain and sorrow.

The most effective way to overcome temptation is to prevent it from entering our hearts. Temptation is powerful because it offers immediate pleasure. When we succumb to impulsive pleasure, we commit wrong actions to cover up or continue the wrongful behavior. Therefore, it is crucial to resist temptation early, before it leads us astray. The longer we wrestle with temptation, the weaker our resistance becomes, and Satan's temptation grows stronger, bringing greater suffering into our lives.

To be better prepared, we should examine the common characteristics of trials. By doing so, we can identify and avoid temptations in advance. Ask yourself the following questions: When are you most vulnerable to temptation? Who was by your side during your most challenging trials? What situations make you more prone to difficulties?

Certain emotional states make us more susceptible to temptation. When we are tired, lonely, bored, depressed, stressed, hurt, angry, or anxious, we are more likely to sin. However, it is not only negative emotions that lead to temptation; positive emotions like pride in our achievements or the joy of spiritual upliftment can also be deceptive. The quicker we identify the emotions that make us vulnerable, the better prepared we will be to resist or avoid temptation.

When faced with trials, fear may arise, and we must not succumb to it. As John F. Milburn (1880-1951) said, "Fear is like fire: if controlled, it can help you; if uncontrolled, it will rise up and destroy you."

We must overcome small bad habits associated with minor trials before facing more severe habits and the accompanying greater trials. Every time the impulse of a bad habit arises, we must fight it before it gains control, before it becomes a bigger problem. It is crucial to understand that God is always waiting for us to call upon Him. We must seek His help. God provides the conditions to overcome temptation for those who seek His grace. Therefore, we must not be too proud to seek His help. Often, we believe that we know what is best for us better than God, which prevents us from seeking His help, ultimately leading to failure. By honestly examining our lives, we can see recurring patterns and temptations. This realization should motivate us to seek God's help. Trials and tribulations can also be beneficial, making us realize the transience of life. Everything we build, believe in, and achieve on this earth is not permanent.

Overcoming trials also teaches us valuable lessons. When actions made with good intentions are misunderstood, we learn humility and forgiveness and seek God's guidance to reconcile with our neighbors. Keeping our faith strong and relying on God is crucial in enduring and overcoming trials.

# 21.
# The Power of Gratitude

In our daily lives, we navigate through over 6,000 thoughts, with two-thirds being negative and one-third positive. The challenge arises when we let negative thoughts exert control, leading to resentment, complaints, anger, envy, jealousy, division, fear, doubt, and a weakening of our spirit—ultimately robbing us of happiness. It's within our power to choose whether each day will be lived with difficulty or happiness.

The true sources of distress are not external, but internal. Regardless of external circumstances, a person attains happiness by maintaining a relaxed and comfortable mind, fulfilling human duties, and embracing a contented life.

Discovering a minimum of ten daily reasons for gratitude and expressing thanks cultivates joy and happiness. The repetition of acknowledging and appreciating conditions fosters a positive habit, enhancing the richness of your daily life.

Conflicts arising from human relationships can be difficult for us. Lack of communication, misunderstanding, and discord can cause internal stress. Additionally, unconditional expectations of oneself and perfectionism can add to the burden. By considering these aspects, you can find ways to maintain inner composure even in difficult situations.

The impact of thoughts on our lives is significant; hence, minimizing negative thoughts and nurturing a positive mindset is crucial. Many concerns that trouble us often originate from within, but with inner strength, any challenge can be overcome. Engaging in the practice of gratitude proves to be a beneficial habit, enhancing the richness of our daily lives.

A person with a consistently grateful heart embodies positivity, enabling them to accomplish tasks, while an individual lacking gratitude becomes hindered by a negative mindset, rendering them incapable. Gratitude, declared as the secret to happiness, is eloquently endorsed by the Talmud, stating, "The wisest person is a learner, and the happiest person lives with gratitude." This principle transcends ownership, with true happiness found in appreciating what one has rather than complaining about what is lacking.

Happiness, the byproduct of gratitude, enters through the door of thankfulness and departs when complaints arise. The correlation between happiness and gratitude is evident: to be happy, one must be grateful, and the magnitude of happiness corresponds to the depth of gratitude. Expressing gratitude for both small and lacking aspects yields significant returns, transforming deficiencies into abundance. Gratitude not only resolves problems but also enhances relationships, fostering happiness, health, and strength.

Thankfulness acts as a vessel for God's grace, blessings, joy, and happiness. Cultivating gratitude towards God, people, and all aspects of life initiates a ripple effect of happiness—first within oneself, then extending to others and the surrounding community. The vessel of gratitude becomes a receptacle for divine grace, enriching lives with blessings and fostering joy and happiness.

Greek philosopher Aristotle wisely stated, "Happiness belongs to the grateful," emphasizing that the happiest individual is not defined by material possessions but by a profound sense of gratitude. The essence of happiness transcends mere ownership, as a heart devoid of gratitude resembles hell, and a person lacking gratitude is akin to a dry wilderness.

Gratitude, a quiet force with profound influence across all aspects of our lives, shares a resemblance to the silent yet powerful nature of the sun radiating heat, Earth's gravitational force maintaining order, and dew falling at night to bring vitality and beauty to plants. Among the languages spoken by humans, none holds greater blessing than the simple phrase 'thank you.' As our gratitude increases, so does the richness and happiness in our lives.

# 22.
# Let's pray even when we are busy

Prayer is a spiritual breath attained through personal communication with God, and it stands as the ultimate means to nurture an intimate relationship with Him. Just as we require physical sustenance, our spiritual improvement also necessitates nourishment. The busier we become in the world, the more imperative it becomes to engage in prayer.

When we pray, our Heavenly Father in heaven hears and responds to our entreaties. God answers our prayers when it aligns with what is most advantageous. Spiritual power emerges solely through the act of prayer. Much like breathing, daily prayer can become ingrained in our lives, evolving into a natural habit that empowers our connection with God.

Similar to steam amassing to form clouds and culminating in rainfall, consistent prayer accumulates in the realm of the divine, where God, who recalls our prayers, inevitably answers in His distinctive and enigmatic manner.

Thus, we must embrace prayer as an ingrained practice. God, being the ultimate problem-solver, can provide solutions through prayer. By presenting our troubles through prayer, we invoke a healing force that aids in resolving issues. When we openly seek solace for our weaknesses, pain, and suffering, our spirits intertwine with God's, leading to healing and unearthing untapped strength. Those who maintain a habit of prayer attain spiritual power and authority. Prayerful individuals establish a connection to heavenly authority and receive spiritual empowerment from God.

"For the word of God is living and active, sharper than any two-edged sword, piercing to the division of soul and of spirit, of joints and of marrow, and discerning the thoughts and intentions of the heart. And no creature is hidden from his sight, but all are naked and exposed to the eyes of him to whom we must give account."(Hebrews 4 : 13)

"Call to me and I will answer you, and will tell you great and hidden things that you have not known."(Jeremiah 33 : 3)

Daniel exemplified a life of prayer. Despite being among the Judahites taken captive to Babylon, he resolved to pray thrice daily to God. He maintained his integrity even during three years of royal education, abstaining from indulgent fare. Trusting God unwaveringly, he encountered angels, not lions, when thrown into the den. Daniel's prosperous life stemmed from trust in God, adherence to His Word, and a prayerful existence amid hardships.

In his book "Prayer," Richard Foster describes the development of prayer in four stages through sustained practice. The first stage involves external discipline, requiring continuous effort for mastery. In the second stage, prayer enters the subconscious. The third stage sees prayer taking root in the heart, transcending intellect. In the fourth stage, prayer permeates the entire being, becoming a natural and pervasive rhythm.

Abraham Lincoln (1809-65) was a man who prayed more fervently during his busiest times. His entire life was a testament to a devout prayerful existence. Preferring to trust in God over his own abilities, he maintained an unwavering commitment to prayer from his earliest years.

The key to his success in navigating the Civil War, stemming from a divided national sentiment, lay in his steadfast faith. He clung to his unwavering conviction of triumph, anchored by his reliance on God, even amidst situations where victory seemed elusive. President Lincoln's victory hinged not on military might, but on his sincere dedication to prayer and dependence on God.

As the Union Army faced retreat to the defense line around Washington, D.C., due to a lack of competent leaders and an undisciplined militia, Lincoln fervently entreated God for the wisdom to navigate this crisis.

His capacity to unite a fractured public and maintain unwavering resolve in the presence of extremist viewpoints emanated from his identity as a man of prayer, driven by a profound yearning to relinquish personal desires and harmonize with the divine will.

George Mueller, a devout man of prayer, asserted, "God never forsakes a praying individual." Throughout the Bible, those who cried out and prayed received answers and solutions. The potency of prayer is immense—a spiritual conduit connecting us with God.

By engaging in continuous prayer, we acquire spiritual authority, and in due course, God responds to our prayers at the most fitting moment.

# 23.
# The Path to a Prosperous Life

Every morning, we begin our day full of challenges. If we start the day by focusing only on problems, we end up living tired and overwhelmed. However, if we start the day by meditating on God's Word, we gain new strength, leading to a positive life. Those who live with positive thoughts about possibilities, creative ideas, dreams, hope, courage, joy, abundance, gratitude, and happiness live prosperous and victorious lives. When facing adversity, we must hold on to hope, believe in God's greatness, and embrace a vision.

The key to living a prosperous life lies in our connection with God. This can be seen in biblical figures like Daniel and Joseph.

Daniel, although taken as a captive from Judah to Babylon, lived a prosperous life through unwavering faith. His commitment to praying three times a day and maintaining a pure life made him stand out. Even in the lions' den, Daniel's trust in God allowed him to see angels instead of roaring lions, enabling him to prosper even in difficulties.

Joseph's life was also prosperous. Joseph was a dreamer. Despite being hated by his brothers for sharing dreams where they would bow to him, and being sold to Egypt at the young age of seventeen, Joseph maintained hope and trust in God through his trials. Even when unjustly imprisoned, the Lord was with him. When Joseph became the Prime Minister of Egypt at thirty, Pharaoh said, "Can we find anyone like this man, one in whom is the spirit of God?" Joseph trusted God, overcoming his trials and living a prosperous life.

In our environment, difficulties and trials are inevitable. Overcoming fear with courage and having absolute trust in God are crucial for a prosperous life. C.S. Lewis, famous for 'The Chronicles of Narnia', emphasized in 'The Problem of Pain' that living obediently to God is the shortcut to a prosperous life.

Pain is synonymous with 'suffering', 'anguish', 'tribulation', 'adversity', or 'problems', and the problem of pain concerns these. The right good for creatures is to surrender themselves to their Creator. When they do so, creatures are good and happy. When the will bestowed by the Creator returns in joy to obedience, there is heaven and the Holy Spirit. The problem in our current world is how to recover this self-surrender. The question of why our healing must be painful can be answered by understanding that returning a will we have so long claimed as our own is inherently painful, no matter where or how it happens.

In a fiercely competitive society, relying solely on oneself leads to deep frustration. Life becomes empty and vain without God. Drawing closer to God is important.

To live a prosperous life, it is essential to be with God. A life filled with joy, gratitude, peace, and happiness is a life that leads to prosperity. Trusting and obeying God, following His guidance, and living with inner strength, spiritual ability, and spiritual authority lead us to prosperity.

Living as a light that brightens the darkness and as the salt of the earth, being wise and humble, and having a positive influence on the world is the way to live a prosperous life. Just like a tree planted by streams of water, with leaves that are always green and lush, living with pride, gratitude, joy, and hope as God's children every day, and relying on and obeying the Lord, He will lead us to a prosperous life filled with blessings and grace.

# 24.
# Living with the End in Mind

Every human being will face death. Life is a continuous journey towards that inevitable end. Contemplating death instills humility in our existence.

Our time in this world is brief. Therefore, we must live each day to the fullest. Don't dwell on past failures; instead, focus on the present and maintain hope for the future. By doing so, you can fill each day with purpose and meaning.

The great Russian author Leo Tolstoy is best known for his epic novel War and Peace. However, less known is his short story The Three Questions (1903). At the heart of this story are questions posed by a king seeking the meaning of life:

- When is the right time to do something?
- Now. It is the only time we have control over.
- Who is the most important person?
- The person in front of us, because we may never have the chance to meet another.
- What is the most important task?
- To do good to the person we are with in the present moment, as that is the purpose for which we were created.

You might have heard the saying, "There is no time like the present." This means we should not put off until tomorrow what we can do today. As mentioned earlier, we are less aware of the limited time we have when we are young. We often think of death as something far off, pushing it out of our minds and returning to our familiar routines. However, the truth is that none of us knows when or how our last day will come. Therefore, our lives should be about making the most of the time God has given us. Welcoming each new day is one of the most inspiring and exciting experiences in life. If we treat every day as our last, bring God's kingdom to earth, love our neighbors, and glorify God, we will truly live a fulfilling life.

Ancient philosophers distinguished between two types of time: chronos, which measures our days and years, and kairos, which is God's eternal time. On earth, we live within the narrow window of chronos time that God has granted us. However, we will spend eternity (kairos) with God in heaven.

God has given us the gift of free will, allowing us to choose how to use our time. We have the freedom to serve God or to serve ourselves. But as we read in Ecclesiastes, the ultimate authority is clear:

"For everything there is a season, and a time for every matter under heaven: a time to be born, and a time to die; a time to plant, and a time to pluck up what is planted; a time to kill, and a time to heal; a time to break down, and a time to build up; a time to weep, and a time to laugh; a time to mourn, and a time to dance; a time to cast away stones, and a time to gather stones together; a time to embrace, and a time to refrain from embracing; a time to seek, and a time to lose; a time to keep, and a time to cast away; a time to tear, and a time to sew; a time to keep silence, and a time to speak; a time to love, and a time to hate; a time for war, and a time for peace. I perceived that there is nothing better for them than to be joyful and to do good as long as they live; also that everyone should eat and drink and take pleasure in all his toil—this is God's gift to man. I perceived that whatever God does endures forever; nothing can be added to it, nor anything taken from it. God has done it, so that people fear before him."(Ecclesiastes 3 :1-8,12-14)

According to John Calvin (1509-1564), without the hope of eternity after death, we are no better than beasts. This is because a life that does not consider death remains in a state of perpetual ignorance. Conversely, living with the end in mind ensures that no day is wasted. Instead, we can reflect on whether we are living righteously.

Always remember, life is a precious gift from God entrusted to us for a brief period. It is our duty to use the time we have to the fullest, glorifying and honoring God by loving one another.

# Section Five:
## Opening The Portal of Happiness

# 25.
# Navigating Adversity: Finding Strength and Resilience

Life is a continuous series of challenges and adversities, and our journey is filled with unexpected obstacles and trials. Yet, even in the depths of despair, we can discover remarkable strength and resilience.

In my early thirties, the business I had invested all my savings in was completely destroyed by an unexpected building fire, leaving me penniless overnight. At that time, it felt like I was trapped in endless darkness and despair. However, even in that moment, I decided not to give up. I realized that I had to be the one to lift myself up.

The first step towards recovery was believing in myself. I also had unwavering faith that the Lord was always with me. My situation and circumstances were far from easy, and it took several years of immense hardship to stand back up, but I eventually did.

Additionally, the love and support from those around me were a great source of strength. My family and friends continuously encouraged me, and their warm words and actions comforted and gave me courage. There were moments when I felt weak, but during those times, the support from those around me gave me the strength to rise again.

The greatest lesson I learned from overcoming adversity was resilience. Resilience is not merely enduring difficulties but learning and growing from them, surpassing one's limits, and discovering new possibilities within adversity. Moreover, failures and setbacks make us stronger. The important thing is to never give up and to keep moving forward.

My heart has become much stronger than before, and now, I am no longer afraid of any difficulty. Adversity tests us, but through it, we can discover and grow. The key is to believe in our strength and resilience throughout the process and to keep moving forward relentlessly.

Life occasionally throws us tough challenges. However, through these challenges, we can discover our true selves and move toward a better future. The strength and resilience gained from overcoming adversity make us stronger and brighten our lives.

We faced an incredibly tough period worldwide due to the COVID-19 pandemic, with millions of deaths. After the World Health Organization declared COVID-19 a global pandemic on March 11, 2020, we faced immense adversity but eventually managed to cope and overcome the disease. The leaders who navigated the complexities of the COVID-19 pandemic will be remembered as pioneers who overcame tremendous difficulties and healed the world. Their resilience inspires us greatly, and we commend their courage in overcoming adversity.

Whether individuals, organizations, or nations, when faced with adversity, it can seem difficult and frightening to overcome. However, if we seize it as an opportunity to reframe our strength to overcome hardship, we can change our perspective and gain the power to keep moving forward. Even in the face of seemingly insurmountable obstacles, continuous effort will help us build the strength and resilience to move forward.

Challenge, dedication, courage, love, and humility play fundamental roles in overcoming adversity. Ultimately, our attitude toward adversity determines our ability to overcome it. Approaching challenges with a positive and hopeful mindset, along with preparation and adaptability, forms the foundation of resilience. Therefore, we must always face adversity with optimism and determination, recognizing that every challenge contains opportunities for growth and strength, and we must develop our strength and resilience when faced with adversity.

# 26.
# God's Power through My Weakness

God prefers to use individuals who acknowledge and embrace their weaknesses. Every person possesses weaknesses, yet we often attempt to deny, defend, or conceal them, hindering God from using them as He intends. However, God perceives our weaknesses differently. Weaknesses encompass limitations that we either inherit or lack the power to alter. These limitations may manifest as physical disabilities, chronic illnesses, diminished stamina, or reduced abilities. They can also appear as emotional scars, tragic memories, character flaws, genetic predispositions, or limitations in talent and intelligence. It's essential to recognize that not everyone is naturally gifted or talented in the same way.

Reflecting on the limitations in my life, it's easy to feel that I can never be of use to God. However, it's crucial to understand that God isn't constrained by our limitations; rather, He delights in infusing His great power into ordinary vessels.

Moreover, our weaknesses serve to amplify our compassion for others and our capacity for ministry. They cultivate within us a deeper empathy and understanding of others' struggles. God desires us to engage in ministry reflective of Christ's example on earth, where our vulnerabilities become avenues for healing and connection.

In fact, our most profound life messages and impactful ministries often stem from our deepest wounds—the very aspects we may feel ashamed of or hesitant to share with others. These vulnerabilities, when embraced, become potent tools in God's hands for bringing healing and restoration to others.

Throughout the Bible, we encounter numerous instances where God's chosen servants were individuals considered weak by societal standards. God demonstrates His prowess in transforming weaknesses into strengths, affirming His desire to take our greatest vulnerabilities and turn them into sources of power and testimony.

Embarking on ministry journeys from a place of vulnerability is fundamental. As we lower our defenses, discard our masks, and share our pain, we create space for God to work through us in serving others. Granted, acknowledging our weaknesses can feel daunting. It requires us to relinquish our shields and open ourselves up to potential rejection. Yet, the rewards outweigh the risks.

Embracing vulnerability grants emotional liberation. By laying bare our experiences, we alleviate stress and confront our fears head-on, paving the way for personal freedom. Furthermore, humility isn't about downplaying our strengths or diminishing ourselves; it's about candidly acknowledging our weaknesses. Authenticity invites God's grace to permeate our lives, fostering a reciprocal exchange of grace among others.

Weakness, far from being a flaw, exudes a captivating allure. Humility draws people closer, while arrogance serves as a deterrent. Honesty acts as a beacon, attracting genuine connections. Indeed, vulnerability is the conduit to deep intimacy, a gateway through which meaningful relationships are nurtured and sustained.

God's desire to utilize our weaknesses alongside our strengths is profound. When others only witness our strengths, it may evoke frustration or even intimidation. However, when they observe God working through us despite our vulnerabilities, it serves as a source of encouragement and inspiration.

Strengths often breed competition, fostering comparisons and divisions. Conversely, weaknesses foster a sense of community and unity. They remind us of our shared humanity and reliance on God's grace. Through our weaknesses, we find solidarity with others, forming bonds that transcend individual capabilities and achievements. In embracing our weaknesses, we cultivate an environment where God's power shines through our imperfections, fostering a spirit of collaboration and mutual support.

In our journey, we reach a pivotal juncture where we must choose between merely impressing others and genuinely influencing them. While it's possible to create a favorable impression from a distance, true influence necessitates closeness and authenticity. As we draw near, our flaws inevitably come into view. However, the hallmark of effective leadership isn't flawless perfection but unwavering reliability.

Trust forms the bedrock of leadership. People gravitate towards leaders they can rely on, whose words and actions align with integrity. Authenticity fosters trust; pretending to be perfect erodes it. Therefore, it's imperative to acknowledge our weaknesses openly and embrace them with pride. By demonstrating vulnerability and honesty, we cultivate trust and forge meaningful connections that transcend superficial impressions.

God wants to accept and use our weaknesses. Instead of being limited by our constraints, He wants to pour great power into ordinary, humble, and sincere vessels, and use those who fully trust in Him.

# 27.
# Choice of Thoughts, Power of Thoughts, and Value of Thoughts

People grapple with myriad thoughts each day because continuous thinking is intrinsic to human existence. True human existence emerges when one lives while contemplating thoughts, a concept underscored by the assertion that 90% of human behavior is governed by the unconscious, with most individuals focusing only on the surface 10%, as outlined in Daniel Kahneman's "Thinking, Fast and Slow" (2013). Unfortunately, the unconscious can be tainted by detrimental information, leading to feelings of giving up or eventual failure. To counteract this, it becomes imperative to shift the realm of consciousness towards an environment that fosters positive information. Instances of spontaneously solving problems or generating ideas during a stroll exemplify the positive outcomes resulting from the fusion created by our unconscious mind, akin to a 24-hour active computer. By deliberately inputting positive information into the unconscious, favorable results can be attained. Thus, enhancing decision-making skills becomes pivotal to selectively embrace positive information relevant to one's goals, utilizing the unconscious mind as a guide to achieving desired objectives.

## Choice of Thoughts

Our thoughts serve as the origin of all our actions, guiding our lives. At the crossroads of life, whether faced with significant or trivial matters, we make choices that shape our destiny. Upon meeting someone for the first time, as suggested by Malcolm Gladwell's "Blink" theory, judgments are formed within two seconds. This rapid decision-making extends to emergency situations, where intellectual senses developed in moments guide our actions, enhancing agility through knowledge accumulation. In a swiftly changing world, embracing change and adeptly navigating emerging trends are essential; stagnation leads to retreat. The speed of our thoughts dictates our choice of thoughts, influencing decisions in the digital age. Understanding the flow of information is paramount, particularly in an internet landscape where quick thinking and decision-making prevail.

## Power of Thoughts

In ancient anthropology, humans were termed Homo sapiens, denoting "thinking persons." The mastery of all creation by humans lies in their ability to think—the power of thoughts, where stronger thoughts hold greater value. A tale from Aesop's fables recounts a donkey scenario where indecisiveness reflects a loss of the power of thought and a deficiency in the value of thoughts.

The power of thoughts encompasses faith, confidence, infinite potential, courage, hope, and vision. Maturing through trials, it flourishes in adversity. Historical figures like Dante, Milton, Marco Polo, and Admiral Nelson exemplify the triumph of thought in the face of challenges, altering the course of history. Dante, after 20 years of difficult wandering, wrote "Divine Comedy." Milton, blind and in pain, penned "Paradise Lost." Marco Polo, imprisoned, dictated "Explorations in the East," sparking European interest in the East. Admiral Nelson, despite severe injuries, led a victorious battle in 1805, changing history.

Even amid adversity, the power of thoughts enables a victorious life. It harbors infinite possibilities, steering lives positively.

## Value of Thoughts

Angela E. Hunt's "The Tale of the Three Trees" illustrates life's worth. The olive tree, oak tree, and pine tree each had grand dreams. The olive tree dreamed of becoming a beautiful jewelry box but became a trough. The oak tree wished to carry a king but became a small, shabby ship. The pine tree sought a high place but was struck by lightning and discarded. However, the olive tree became the manger for baby Jesus, the oak tree carried Jesus, and the pine tree became the cross of Jesus. Despite their altered dreams, these trees played crucial roles in significant events, emphasizing the true value of thought. Recognizing God's grand plan underscores our intrinsic value and potential.

Living a worthwhile life involves contemplating the profound message in Hunt's tale. Though we may perceive ourselves as small, God's plan for us reflects our true value—the essence of thought. Comparisons breed unhappiness; individual worth lies in cultivating unique thoughts. Wise individuals rely on internal judgment, guarding their hearts. Nurturing the power of thoughts, broadening intellectual senses, and enhancing the value of genuine thoughts shape a worthwhile life.

# 28.
# New Year Wishes

The dawn of the new year is upon us, bringing with it expectations and hopes. As the New Year unfolds, individuals carry within their hearts a wish for the upcoming year. Hope, the belief that something will come true, becomes a powerful force that enables us to overcome difficulties. Without hope, our ability to navigate this world is diminished. With hope, one can surmount challenges and find happiness, shaping a future dependent on our thoughts, while the past remains immutable.

May this new year usher in an abundance of knowledge.

Asking astrophysicists about the universe reveals a vast expanse of unknowns exceeding their knowns. The knowledge we must amass while residing in this world extends beyond astrophysics, encompassing philosophy, literature, theology, science, history, medicine, law, politics, management, linguistics, education, music, and art. In the era of artificial intelligence, characterized by data reliance, AI is swiftly evolving as the linchpin of the 4th Industrial Revolution, deeply ingrained in our lives and acclaimed as the prime asset of the 21st century. Already integrated into numerous professional domains, it is imperative to comprehend its effective utilization. Furthermore, a commitment to continuous learning and expanding knowledge across diverse fields is essential.

May this new year bestow upon us greater patience.

Bao chestnut trees, originating from Madagascar in Africa, require 20 years to reach flowering and 60 years before bearing fruit, with a lifespan extending for thousands of years. Steadfast pursuit of our dreams, the nurturing of hopes, and continuous progress are essential, demanding perseverance in the face of difficulties. To escape the busyness of daily life, where we often lose sight of our surroundings, it is crucial to prioritize rest when fatigued and consistently make time for exercise to maintain our health. Instead of rushing tirelessly toward our goals, slowing down, practicing patience, humility, and persistent movement are keys to success.

In the new year, let us broaden the horizons of our lives.

To expand the horizons of life, transcending our environment is imperative. Adopting a broad perspective toward the world is the first step. An open heart, capable of embracing even the universe, significantly influences the quality and value of our lives. Enriching our minds with a rich imagination, demonstrating courage to challenge fears, and nurturing tireless passion unlock infinite possibilities. By broadening our horizons and aiming higher, life's boundaries and areas will expand, enabling continuous growth, positive influence on the world, and a creative existence.

In the new year, may we cultivate deeper love for our neighbors.

Recognizing that the most precious person is oneself, self-love becomes a foundation. Living with love involves being considerate of neighbors, sharing courage, hope, and joy, and blessing them. Wishing for the disappearance of sorrow, pain, and suffering caused by wars and diseases, envisioning a reconciled and peaceful world is our hope. Aspiring to become a harmonious society through tolerance, encouragement, forgiveness, and love, rather than discord, division, hatred, and jealousy, shapes our collective vision. The flow of love, transforming a dry world into warmth and beauty, is a shared aspiration.

May this new year bring us more knowledge, greater patience, broader horizons of life, and deeper love for our neighbors. May it empower us to overcome the worries, anxiety, nervousness, despair, sadness, and frustration that pervade the world, allowing us to live with pride, joy, gratitude, hope, love, and passion. Let there be an eternal longing for eternity and sincere appreciation for the beauty created in time, enriched by heavenly spiritual things. Approaching everyday life with an active and positive mind, gratitude, and hope, let us recognize it as a blessed moment containing the truth of life. Grateful for everything we have been given, may today surpass yesterday, guiding us toward becoming the best version of ourselves.

# 29.
# The Sound of Spring

In spring, the breath of life can be felt as everything comes to life anew. Just imagining spring rejuvenates everyone. Spring brims with vitality, injecting vigor and momentum into life. Unlike the withering sight beneath the thawing ice, spring brings forth a refreshing and vibrant renewal.

Like the hopeful heart of a farmer stepping out into the morning sun, spring bestows hope upon us. This resilience stems from the patience endured through dark winters. True vitality cannot be achieved without enduring pain and hardship. Just as the sincerity poured into great works of art is evident, so too is the resilience required to create them.

Even the branches, once shriveled in the past winter, awaken with new life. Seeds sprout with dreams, and birds find warm earth to reveal new forms. Spring overflows with hope. Past sorrows are buried beneath the soil, replaced by love and purity. Spring is more cherished than smiling flowers, naturally sweeping away the dust of time.

Listening to Vivaldi's "Four Seasons," one can hear spring singing and dancing joyfully. This melody unveils the sound of spring. With the arrival of the warm season, birds joyfully sing in the morning, and streams whisper gently as melodies bloom within the atmosphere of spring.

Even in nature, the sounds of spring can be heard. Trees sprout new buds at their tips, filled with the vitality of leaves and blossoms. Despite snowstorms and cold, the will to live is strong. The sorrow of spring's departure is felt only by insects that live for a single year. Trees welcome spring again after it passes, just as they do with autumn.

In our lives, spring comes often. Reflecting on these seasons enriches our lives. Spring always finds us and reminds us of the passage of time, though sometimes we fail to hear its call. Dandelions, plum blossoms, magnolias, forsythias, azaleas, cherry blossoms, peach blossoms, roses, lilacs, and the daffodils of spring are abundant blessings. Spring is always true, humble, and never rude. Through its sounds, we come to realize the truths of life.

Spring nurtures life, and in its sounds, we feel the rebirth of life. My dormant soul awakens, and my silent love comes alive again. Spring sings of love. Let us live loving one another. Love is gentle and kind, patient, and neither boasts nor fears. Through the sounds of spring, we come to realize the truths of life.

# 30.
# Opening the Portal of Happiness

The portal of happiness swings both ways—outward and within. In joy, embrace today's sunbeams' gentle warmth. And in sorrow, nurture the stars of tomorrow.

Our lives respire from the world without and within, Mirroring the tides of our life's vast ocean, Where happiness and sorrow ebb and flow incessantly.

Amidst life's trove of memories amassed, Many are the moments of joy, yet Why do they fade so fleetingly, While sorrowful memories endure?

Unable to recall moments of joy, Only the shadows of sorrow linger, Casting a pall over our hearts.

Hence, we strive to reclaim happiness, Smiling amidst tears, Mending wounds with laughter, Effacing sorrowful memories akin to an eraser's touch, Gratefully welcoming joy's return, And stoically embracing sorrow's visitation.

The portal of happiness opens outward and within, For when one portal shuts, another reveals itself. In joy, cherish today's sunbeams' tender glow. And in sorrow, nurture the promise of tomorrow's stars. For the portal of happiness is always open.

# 31.
# You Who Held My Hand

When I lost my direction in the valley of darkness,
You held my hand and walked with me.
When hardships and trials came and I collapsed,
You, who raised me up.
When my mind was exhausted by frustration and despair,
You hugged me warmly,
Sharing my pain, crying together,
You told me that together we can overcome all difficulties.
When a strong wind blows,
It is an unavoidable pain for a tree standing with roots,
But only the twigs shake, while the roots endure.
You grasp my hand, igniting hope's lamp,
Urging strength as we forge ahead.
I'm grateful to have you by my side.

# 32.
# Yesterday, Today, Tomorrow, and Time

Time flows seamlessly through yesterday, today, and tomorrow. Today is a precious present. Yesterday is the past, and tomorrow is the future.
Time, an ever-flowing river, carries us along its currents, molding our experiences and shaping our souls.
In the stillness of the present moment,
we find the intersection of all times. Yesterday's lessons carve the path we tread today, while today's actions sow the seeds of tomorrow's harvest.

To live fully is to honor each moment,
weaving a tapestry of experiences rich and varied.
Let not the shadows of yesterday cloud today's sun,
nor the fears of tomorrow steal today's joy.
In the dance of time, we are both dancers and choreographers,
crafting a life of meaning and purpose.

Thus, we stand at the crossroads of time,
embracing the past, living the present, and welcoming the future.
With hearts full of laughter, minds open to learning,
and spirits infused with hope,
we navigate the river of time,
finding beauty in its ceaseless flow.

# About the Author

**Daniel K. Lee** is a Christian writer and a devoted believer. He earned his degree from the College of Education at Jeonbuk National University in South Korea and an MBA from Atlanta University. After building his career as an educator, he ran a business in Manhattan, New York, for over 30 years, practicing Christian love through community service, donations, and fostering good relationships with others.

In the United States, he participated in ministries to help the homeless and took part in short-term overseas missions, spreading the gospel to indigenous people in Latin America. As an elder of his church, he shared his faith by preaching during Saturday services.

His second book, "A Loving Father's Bequest to His Child" (Korean edition), became a bestseller, and he donated all proceeds to help those in need, continuing to practice love for his neighbors. He consistently strives to make a positive impact on his community through his Christian way of life.

This book was written to share hope, vision, faith, and happiness with readers based on the author's rich experiences and sound values, aiming to guide them how to live a happy and fulfilling life.

www.ingramcontent.com/pod-product-compliance
Lightning Source LLC
LaVergne TN
LVHW051950060526
838201LV00059B/3583